UNDERSTANDING THE CONSTITUTION

Henry Conserva

authorHOUSE®

AuthorHouse™
1663 Liberty Drive
Bloomington, IN 47403
www.authorhouse.com
Phone: 1-800-839-8640

First published by AuthorHouse   8/4/2011

ISBN: 978-1-4634-1383-5 (sc)
ISBN: 978-1-4634-1378-1 (e)

Printed in the United States of America

Any people depicted in stock imagery provided by Thinkstock are models, and such images are being used for illustrative purposes only. Certain stock imagery © Thinkstock.

This book is printed on acid-free paper.

I dedicate this book to the memory of my dear wife Jean F. Dewees. She encouraged me to write this book and provided me with many ideas and suggestions that helped me organize the work. Without her this book would never have been published. With me she co-authored Tips for Teachers and Remarkable California. Her interest in the education of teachers and students motivated her in her writing. Words cannot express how very much I miss her.

Forword

I have taught classes in government (civics) for thirty years, and throughout those thirty years the Constitution was a major topic. At the middle schools in San Francisco, California, where I taught, students in the eighth grade had to pass an objective test on the Constitution. Students had to write down the Preamble to the Constitution from memory and then answer true/false, multiple choice, and matching questions. Rightly or wrongly, I wound up teaching to the test. Rote memorization of facts was the principal method used in preparing students. They were warned that failure to pass the test might keep them from being promoted to the next grade. I had the feeling that we teachers could have been more creative in our teaching. In discussions with my students, I soon became aware that they had not grasped the meaning of the Constitution. They really didn't know the significance of the phrases found in the Preamble, and they didn't seem to know what problems were faced and solved by the delegates to the Constitutional Convention of 1787.

Don't get me wrong. Knowledge of facts is essential, but we shouldn't stop there. I wrote this book in an attempt to give students a broader and deeper perception of constitutional background information, issues confronting delegates, and the general importance of America's plan for government.

This book contains essays that break new ground in explaining the Constitution to students. The essay on the Preamble to the Constitution thoroughly explores each phrase and provides students with background information that clarifies the wording of this introduction to the Constitution. Another essay deals with the concept of power and its importance to a number of decisions and compromises made in this second plan for governing the United States. Other essays discuss other constitutional topics that provide additional insights into the challenges that faced the framers of the Constitution.

The Articles of Confederation have been included for comparative studies so that students can draw their own conclusions about the adequacy or inadequacy of this document.

Several exercises and lessons designed to present factual information are included. Objective answers to exercise questions can be found in the back section of the book.

Some of the quizzes and examinations constitute self-testing activities so that students can assess their progress in mastering constitutional content.

To aid students in interpreting constitutional wording, there is a glossary of terms that helps give eighteenth-century words a twenty-first-century definition.

A Constitutional Topic Locator allows students to quickly determine where various topics are discussed in the Constitution.

For further study, a bibliography of books on the Constitution is provided at the back of the book.

ACKNOWLEDGMENTS

Understanding the Constitution is a book whose beginnings can be traced back to 1954 at A. P. Giannini Junior High School in San Francisco, California. As a new teacher of American history, I was given help, advice, and directions by Ms. Lorraine Palmer, head of the social studies department. I was informed that all of the eighth-grade American history students had to pass a test on the Constitution. It was a major production. The students were told that their promotion to the ninth grade might depend on their passing this test. All eighth-grade American history classes were marched into the school cafeteria and given the test, which lasted over an hour.

This required test got me into the task of teaching about the Constitution intensively. Students were highly motivated and wanted to study hard to pass the test. To tell the truth, I was not very knowledgeable about the fine points of the Constitution at that time, so I began to collect lessons from other teachers. Mr. Richard Murphy and Mr. Roger Johnson gave me some excellent lesson plans. Later, I transferred to J. Eugene McAteer High School in San Francisco; I continued teaching American history and civics (government).

One teacher in particular was a source of many lesson plans and methods for teaching the Constitution to high school students. Mr. Joseph Lewbin suggested an interdisciplinary approach to the study of the document. He showed me how much mathematics was involved in the political decision-making that ran throughout the Constitution.

After years of collecting ideas and lessons on the Constitution, I thought of writing a book on the subject. My goal was to help secondary school and college students to better understand the Constitution. The person who really got me active in working on a manuscript was my wife and book production partner Jean Dewees. She monitored every aspect of my work and made valuable suggestions and revisions. She was and is indispensable, and I thank her profusely.

Some people read selections from the text and suggested additions or deletions. I am especially indebted to Mr. Rino Di Pasqua, Mr. John Weir, Mr. Aldo Disgrazzi, Mr. Richard Murphy, and Mr. Gordon Chalmers.

I also want to commend the librarians of the Sonoma County library system, especially the Central branch in Santa Rosa and the Windsor branch, for helping me locate bibliographic resources. The Santa Rosa Junior College librarians helped me track down materials unavailable in my local public libraries.

CONTENTS

A SYNOPSIS OF CONSTITUTIONAL HISTORY

In 1787, six years after the Revolutionary War, Americans lived in thirteen independent states that were weakly organized into a loose confederation under the nation's first constitution, the Articles of Confederation. Changes were underway that would transform their government from a confederation into a federation.

Problems emerged under the confederation because states acted independently from each other and often against each other. Trade was hampered by high import duties imposed on goods from other states that made their products unduly expensive. Some states with poor financial resources resorted to printing their own paper money without solid backing, which created a damaging inflation. Given these and other problems, many people felt that a strong central government was needed to bring order and prosperity to the country.

In 1786, delegates from several states held a convention at Annapolis, Maryland to discuss solutions to the nation's commercial, financial, and political problems. These delegates submitted a report to Congress calling for a new convention with delegates from every state to revise the Articles of Confederation.

In 1787, seventy-four delegates from twelve states (Rhode Island refused to send a delegation) met at a constitutional convention in Philadelphia's State House. George Washington was chosen as the presiding officer of the contentious group of delegates.

Many conflicting ideas were proposed at the convention. The "Virginia Plan" called for a congress of two houses, one elected by the people and one by their state legislatures. States would be represented according to their wealth and population. A "New Jersey Plan" called for a one-house legislature representing the states but not the people. Alexander Hamilton presented a plan based on the British system of government that won little support. Fierce debates were daily features of the convention, and tempers rose over several divisive issues.

Large and small states struggled over how they would be represented in the Congress. The Connecticut Compromise solved this problem by providing for a House of Representatives, in which states would be represented by their population, and a Senate, in which all states would have equal representation. Large slave-holding states wanted slaves to be counted for purposes of representation, while states with few slaves voiced opposition to the idea. A compromise was reached in which three-fifths of the slave population would be counted.

What had begun as a move to revise the Articles of Confederation ended in the creation of a new document. This transformed the nation from a confederation of states into a federation of states under a vastly more powerful central government.

Finally, after a series of compromises, the Constitution was ratified by the required nine states and became the supreme law of the land.

THE CONSTITUTION OF THE UNITED STATES IS BORN

After the United States won its Revolutionary War in 1783, the government of the new nation faced many problems that could not easily be handled by the existing Articles of Confederation. Law and order had to be enforced, a large public debt had to be paid, taxes had to be collected, and interstate trade had to be regulated. Relations between the United States and Native American tribes as well as foreign nations had to be established.

The central government established under the Articles of Confederation in 1781 was designed to be weak. It was becoming apparent that a stronger central government might be needed. Some powerful statesmen, such as George Washington and Alexander Hamilton, began to consider creating a strong central government rather than maintaining the existing confederation of states.

Some groups opposed the idea of scrapping the Articles of Confederation. Many farmers and planters had amassed considerable debts during the Revolutionary War. They tended to favor a weak central government, inflated currency, and low prices for foreign goods to ease the burden of debt.

However, other groups wanted a strong central government. Land speculators wanted a police force to protect settlers from hostile Native American tribes who were resisting white penetration of their lands. Ship owners wanted protection from pirates on the high seas. Owners of securities that were issued by the Continental Congress wanted a government strong enough to redeem their securities. Bankers wanted a stable currency, protection against paper money of little value, and the defeat of laws postponing payment of debt. Manufacturers wanted protective tariffs to reduce competition from foreign manufacturers.

These powerful groups supported the development of a new constitution with a strong central government which would better meet their needs. In 1787, the demand for change and reform of the American government began to materialize. A convention, or meeting, was called in Philadelphia. Its purpose was to revise the Articles of Confederation. Delegates came from all the states except Rhode Island, which so feared the possible creation of a central government that it refused to participate.

Political leaders such as George Washington, Benjamin Franklin, James Madison, Alexander Hamilton, Gouverneur Morris, and Robert Morris, along with other delegates, proposed scrapping the Articles of Confederation and writing a new Constitution. A popular idea was to establish a federal government, one that joined a central government with the state governments in a cooperative arrangement. There would be three branches of government in the central government: a legislative, or law-making, branch (the Congress); an executive, or law-enforcing, branch (the President); and a judicial branch responsible for explaining the law and providing for just courts of law (the Supreme Court).

Writing the Constitution was no easy task. Many issues divided the states, and without compromise (an agreement reached by each opposing side giving in on some points), the Constitution might have foundered. The most notable compromise is called The Great Compromise or The Connecticut Compromise. States with large populations wanted more representatives in the proposed national legislature than states with smaller populations. Connecticut's delegates proposed that there be equality of representation in an upper house (Senate) and representation in proportion to population in a lower house (House of Representatives).

This compromise was adopted, removing a huge source of discontent among delegates. However, a new problem presented itself. The lower house would have representation based on population. The slave states wanted to count their slaves for purposes of representation. This was unacceptable to the free states (the states with few slaves). Finally, a three-fifths compromise was reached. A slave would be counted as three-fifths of a person for the purpose of determining representation in the House of Representatives.

The slave trade was another issue resolved by compromise. Free states wanted to ban the slave trade, while slave states strongly objected to such a ban. Resolution of this disagreement came when it was agreed that the newly proposed legislature (the Congress), could not prohibit the importation of slaves until 1808, about twenty years after the Constitution would become the supreme law of the land.

After seemingly endless debate, on September 17, 1787, the delegates produced a final draft of the proposed Constitution. Given the travel conditions of late-eighteenth-century America, the ratification process took time, but by July 2, 1788, ten states had ratified the Constitution and it was adopted. It did not go into effect until March 4, 1789. By 1790, all thirteen states had accepted the Constitution as the highest law in the land.

DELEGATES TO THE
CONSTITUTIONAL CONVENTION
WHO SIGNED THE DOCUMENT IN 1787

Connecticut: William S. Johnson (1727–1819), educator, politician; Roger Sherman (1721–1793), businessman, politician, judge

Delaware: Richard Basset (1745–1815), politician, judge; Gunning Bedford, Jr. (1747–1812), lawyer, statesman; Jacob Broom (1752–1810), postmaster, judge, businessman; John Dickinson (1732–1808), lawyer, politician; George Read (1733–1798), lawyer, politician

Georgia: Abraham Baldwin (1754–1807), lawyer, politician; William Few (1748–1828), lawyer, judge, banker, politician

Maryland: James McHenry (1753–1816), doctor, politician; Daniel Carroll (1730–1796), politician; Daniel Jenifer of St. Thomas (1723–1790), politician

Massachusetts: Nathaniel Gorham (1738), merchant, politician; Rufus King (1755–1827), lawyer, politician

New Hampshire: John Langdon (1741–1819), politician; Nicholas Gilman (1755–1814), politician

New Jersey: David Brearly (1745–1790), lawyer, judge; Jonathan Dayton (1760–1824), politician; William Livingston (1723–1790), politician; William Paterson (1745–1806), lawyer, judge

New York: Alexander Hamilton (1755–1804), lawyer, politician

North Carolina: William Blount (1749–1800), politician; Richard D. Spaight (1758–1802), politician; Hugh Williamson (1735–1819), doctor, politician

Pennsylvania: George Clymer (1739–1813), merchant, politician, banker; Thomas Fitzsimons (1741–1811), merchant, politician; Benjamin Franklin (1706–1790), statesman, scientist; Jared Ingersoll (1749–1822), lawyer, judge; Thomas Mifflin (1744–1800), general, politician; Gouverneur Morris

(1752–1816), politician, statesman; Robert Morris (1734–1806), politician; James Wilson (1742–1798), lawyer, judge, professor

South Carolina: Pierce Butler (1744–1822), politician; Charles Pinckney (1757–1824), lawyer; Charles C. Pinckney (1746–1825), statesman, politician; John Rutledge (1739–1800), judge

Virginia: John Blair: (1732–1800), lawyer; James Madison (1751–1836), politician, statesman, president of the United States; George Washington (1732–1799), politician, general, first President of the United States under the Constitution

EXAMINING SOME PHRASES FROM THE CONSTITUTION'S PREAMBLE

The Preamble

We the people of the United States, in order to form a more perfect union, establish justice, insure domestic tranquility, provide for the common defense, promote the general welfare, and secure the blessings of liberty to ourselves and our posterity, do ordain and establish this Constitution for the United States of America.

A preamble is an introduction to a formal document. Many students in all states have had to memorize the preamble to the Constitution for classes on American government. I feel that few of them have a full understanding of the preamble's meaning.

The first phrase of the preamble, *"We the people ...,"* calls for considerable examination. It is true to say that some delegates to the Constitutional Convention felt that "We the states ..." was a far more appropriate phrase than "We the people." These delegates thought that we should be a nation of states and that the powers of the states should not be subject to the will of the masses. The Constitution reflected this view in such matters as the original process of electing senators. At that time, senators were chosen not by a popular vote, as is done today, but by the state legislatures. The electoral college is another example. The President is chosen by electors who are chosen by the states, not by a popular vote of the people. The states' rights view was so strong, especially in the South, that it became an important factor leading to the Civil War. The power struggle between the states and the central government lives on today.

In the writing of the preamble the "we the people" advocates won the day, but the delegates who feared the possible excesses of people in a democratic system must have felt justified by a contemporary event in Europe—the French Revolution. The behavior of the people in the streets of Paris at the start of the revolution fed the fear of "mobocracy," rule by mobs. Many political figures in the United States were reluctant to give direct and unrestricted power to the people.

"We the people" raises another concern. Who are people? The definitions of terms have a habit of changing over time. What today we think of as people, in a political sense, would have been unthinkable and incomprehensible to most members of America's decision-making class at the end of the eighteenth century.

The Constitution allowed each state to set qualifications for voting, providing they did not violate guarantees of the Constitution. As the Constitution was being written, "people" meant voting citizens. But who could vote? The states excluded women, African-American slaves, Native Americans, white males under twenty-one years of age, and white males over twenty-one years of age without property or a reasonable claim to some wealth. (This latter group was enfranchised soon after.) Since the electoral college system was based on state electors, citizens living in the District of Columbia were excluded from voting as they were not living in a state. These exclusionary policies were reflected in the low percentage of the population voting in presidential elections: in 1824, 3.2 percent; in 1828, 9.5 percent; and in 1840, 14.1 percent.

As time has passed, more and more groups of people have been legally allowed to vote through the passing of amendments to the Constitution. The ratification of the fifteenth amendment in 1870 allowed African-American males to vote. Several states obstructed this voting right until recently. In 1920, after more than seventy years of activity by reformers, women got the right to vote, which roughly doubled the size of the voting population of the nation. In 1961, the twenty-third amendment allowed citizens living in Washington, DC, to vote in presidential elections, and in 1971 the twenty-sixth amendment allowed citizens who were at least eighteen years of age to vote.

The second phrase in the preamble, "in order to form a more perfect union," indicates that the Articles of Confederation, the first plan for governing the United States, needed revision. In fact, many political leaders desired a complete replacement. The Articles of Confederation stood as the legal framework for the government of the United States from 1781 to 1789. During this period, the Congress, the only branch of government under the Articles, passed several innovative and important laws. The Northwest Ordinance of 1787 is an excellent example. It provided a simple democratic way for territories to become new states possessing all the rights of the original thirteen states. Still, the weaknesses of government under the Articles led many to seek a system of government with a strong central authority that could successfully address many of the problems faced by the new nation.

Several special interest groups identified serious flaws in the Articles. Here are a few of them:

1. There was no executive branch of government.
2. No system of national courts existed.
3. Trade between and among states could not be regulated.
4. States could be asked for money, but neither the states nor their citizens could be taxed.
5. No uniform currency was issued; states issued their own currencies.
6. States could and did tax each other's goods.
7. Government debts were not paid, and credit nearly vanished as a result.
8. Congress could plan for an army but could not draft the troops.
9. Treaties could be made but not enforced.
10. Congress could not set up a uniform United States tariff; each state made up its own tariff laws.
11. Congress could debate important issues, but a one-third minority could prevent passage of any proposed law.

1

The Constitution was established to address the problems made insolvable under the Articles of Confederation, thereby forming a more perfect union.

The third phrase, "establish justice," resulted in the creation of a judicial branch of government in Article III of the Constitution. A Supreme Court and inferior courts less powerful than the Supreme Court were to be established. District courts, courts of appeal, a Court of International Trade, a United States Claims Court, the Tax Court of the United States, and the Court of Military Appeals are some examples of federal courts organized under the authority of Article III.

A person who loses a case either in a federal court of appeals or in the highest state court may appeal to the Supreme Court, but there is no guarantee that the case will be accepted by that court.

The fourth phrase, "insure domestic tranquility," addressed fears about uprisings by disgruntled citizens against government authority as well as fears about interstate conflicts. Shay's Rebellion is an example of an uprising that increased the demand for a stronger central government than was provided for under the Articles of Confederation.

Many small farmers in Massachusetts faced foreclosure of their property and imprisonment for failing to pay their debts. In 1786, Shay, a supporter of the farmers, led a mob of about six hundred to try to prevent the state court from imposing punishments on the farmers in debt. The rebellion was soon put down by the state militia, but the impact of the event was significant in getting support for reform and revision of the Articles of Confederation, leading to a Constitutional Convention and ultimately a new constitution for the United States.

Article I, Section 8 of the Constitution directly provides for ensuring domestic tranquility by calling upon the state militias (currently called the National Guard) to execute the laws of the United States, suppress insurrection (uprisings), and repel invasions. Congress has given the president the power to decide when an invasion or insurrection exists. The president can call out the National Guard of any state in such emergencies.

The fifth phrase "provide for the common defense" became the basis for creating the armed forces that exist today. The Revolutionary War revealed many difficulties that the government of the new nation faced under the Articles in confronting British military action against American independence.

To fight a war, a nation needs recruits, weapons, and other supplies, but above all it needs money. The Second Continental Congress was at the mercy of the thirteen state governments when it came to recruiting. The central government could not draft troops. The Continental Army relied mainly on volunteers. The states gave money to the congress as they wished, but the national government did not receive as much as it needed to pursue the war. It also couldn't tax its citizens but relied on the states for funds—which, again, were always less than needed. Those who wanted independence from the British might have lost their struggle if it had not been for the material and financial aid of other nations, especially France, the Netherlands, and Spain.

In spite of all this, the Congress couldn't adequately pay the troops and had to offer free land as an inducement to continue in the Continental Army. About 25 percent of the army toward the end of the war were African Americans, including slaves who were promised freedom in return for their military service.

Article I, Section 8 of the Constitution gives the Congress the power to lay and collect taxes, duties (taxes on imports), and excises (taxes on certain commodities, such as tobacco and liquor) to pay the debts and to provide for the common defenses and general welfare of the United States. Article I, Section 8 also gives the Congress the power to raise and support armies and to provide and maintain a navy.

During the Revolutionary War, it was difficult to provide for the common defense because state militias were mostly concerned with the defense of their own states. The Constitution corrected this difficulty.

The sixth phrase, "to promote the general welfare," was designed to encourage the enactment of laws that would help the economy of the nation and improve the lives of the American people. Article I, Section 8 of the Constitution specifically calls for tax money to be used to promote the general welfare.

The last part of Section 8 is often called the "necessary and proper" clause or the "elastic clause." It states that the Congress can deal with matters not specifically mentioned in the Constitution. The use of the "elastic clause" has aided the Congress in passing laws that promote the welfare of the nation and its people without going through a lengthy process of passing amendments to the Constitution, which can take years to gain final approval.

Section 8 lists several powers of Congress that promote the general welfare. I'm convinced that one of the most significant is the one that called upon the Congress to promote the progress of science and useful arts by securing for authors and inventors the exclusive right to their respective writings and discoveries for limited times. This provision fueled an economic and cultural expansion without parallel.

The seventh of the Preamble's phrases reads, "secure the blessings of liberty to ourselves and our posterity." The term "blessings" can be defined as anything promoting or contributing to happiness, well-being, or prosperity. Liberty and freedom were highly valued by the writers of the Constitution, but not to be enjoyed by all the people: just white males twenty-one years of age or older who owned property or had some wealth. One wonders whether the political leaders of the late eighteenth century ever imagined that their posterity (future generations) would be as inclusive as they are today.

The Constitution of the United States, adopted in 1789, contained few personal guarantees of liberty. The first ten amendments to the Constitution, known as the Bill of Rights, were ratified in 1791. The first eight of those ten amendments guaranteed specific rights and freedoms. Other freedom-granting amendments would follow. Here is a listing of amendments that have expanded the rights and freedoms of the American people. The wording has been updated to include both genders.

Amendment 1—ratified 1791

The Congress may not make laws interfering with the freedoms of religion, speech, the press, assembly, and petition.

Amendment 2—ratified 1791

Right to bear arms

Amendment 3—ratified 1791

Troops cannot be housed in private homes during peacetime

Amendment 4—ratified 1791

People are protected against unreasonable searches and seizures

Amendment 5—ratified 1791

A person cannot be tried for a crime punishable by death unless charged by a grand jury, be tried twice for the same crime, or be forced to testify against himself or herself. A person may not be deprived of life, liberty, or property, except by lawful means. The government must pay a fair price for property taken for public use.

Amendment 6—ratified 1791

A person accused of a crime has a right to a speedy public trial by jury, information about the accusation, help from the court in bringing favorable witnesses to the trial, and the aid of a lawyer.

Amendment 7—ratified 1791

In civil lawsuits involving more than $20, the right to a jury trial is guaranteed.

Amendment 8—ratified 1791

Bails, fines, and punishments cannot be unreasonable.

Amendment 13—ratified 1865

Slavery abolished

Amendment 14—ratified 1868

All people born or naturalized in the United States are citizens. This provision made African Americans citizens. No state may infringe on the rights of citizens of the United States. This provision was designed to make sure black males could not be denied the right to vote on the basis of their race alone. If a state prevents certain citizens from voting, that state's representation in Congress may be reduced. If a federal office holder goes against the oath of office and rebels against the country or helps its enemies, that person cannot ever hold a federal office again. Congress may, however, allow such a person to hold office if two thirds of each house agrees. All debts of the Confederate States are declared invalid and may not be paid.

Amendment 15—ratified 1870

African American suffrage

Amendment 17—ratified 1913

Direct election of senators

Amendment 19—ratified 1920

Women's suffrage

Amendment 23—ratified 1961

Suffrage in the District of Columbia

Amendment 24—ratified 1964

No citizen can be made to pay a tax for the right to vote in a federal election.

Amendment 26—ratified 1971

Suffrage for eighteen-year-olds.

The Preamble that we read first in the original Constitution was written last. The Constitutional Convention's Committee of Style was given the responsibility for composing the Constitution. The authorship of the preamble is attributed to Gouverneur Morris of New York. Much of the credit for the wording in the Constitution belongs to him.

THE FRAMERS OF THE CONSTITUTION WRESTLED WITH SEVERAL QUESTIONS OF POWER. THE STRUGGLE OVER POWER IS A NEVER-ENDING FEATURE OF POLITICAL LIFE.

Power is the ability or official capacity to execute control. Power has been seen as dangerous when it is concentrated in the hands of an individual or group with few or no checks on its use. Many political leaders at the Constitutional Convention would most likely have agreed with the sentiments of Lord Acton, who in 1887 said, "Power tends to corrupt and absolute power tends to corrupt absolutely."

HOW CAN POWER BE REGULATED AND CONTROLLED SO AS TO PREVENT THE RISE OF TYRANNY?

The prevention of the rise of a tyranny or a dictatorship was a central goal of many constitutional delegates. In the search for solutions to the problem of how power can be limited and controlled, few people have been as influential as the French political philosopher Montesquieu. His book *The Spirit of the Laws* (1748) has made an impact on constitutions around the world and especially the Constitution of the United States. Montesquieu believed that political liberty involved separating the legislative, executive, and judicial powers of government. This idea of the separation of these powers was embedded into the Constitution. The legislative, executive and judicial branches had their own powers. In addition, the separation of powers principle was extended by the division of the legislative branch of government into a Senate and a House of Representatives, each having shared as well as exclusive powers.

Concerns about power were far-reaching. Care was taken to protect the rights and powers of small states by creating a Senate in which all states had equal representation, regardless of the size of their populations. Also, the two-thirds vote required in the Senate for the approval of treaties and appointment of some government officials reflects concern about a tyranny of the majority.

It was generally thought dangerous to grant too much power to the people. Until the seventeenth amendment was passed in 1913, senators were to be indirectly elected by their respective state legislatures. The President was to be indirectly elected by an electoral college chosen as the state legislatures decided. The prospect of presidential election by a majority vote of the people was rejected.

It should be noted that the writers of the Constitution made no provision for such radical ideas, for the times, as the initiative (the right of voters to propose laws), the referendum (the right of voters to accept or reject laws), or the recall (the right of voters to remove elected officials from office). These ideas came to life in the Progressive Period in American history, which began in the late nineteenth century and extended into the early twentieth century. These ideas have now been accepted by several states and many local governments, but not by the federal government. The vast majority of the world's nations have rejected these radical reforms for their central governments, with the exceptions of Switzerland, Australia, and New Zealand.

A great concern of the delegates was how power would be shared between the central government and the states. The central government was specifically denied certain powers by the Constitution's Article I, Section 9. The central government could not suspend the writ of habeas corpus (protection against unlawful restraint) except during rebellion or invasion. For example, a suspected spy normally could not be imprisoned except in times of rebellion or invasion. The central government could not pass ex post facto laws (retroactive punishment). The central government could not tax exports from a single state or favor one port over another, and it could not grant titles of nobility. The states were also denied certain powers in Article I, Section 10. They could not pass the aforementioned laws forbidden to the central government. They could not pass import or export duties or create laws impairing the obligation of contracts.

In order to curb any possible abuses of power by one branch of government or two branches working together, an elaborate system of checks on power and balances of power was written into the Constitution. This system of checks and balances went beyond relations among the legislative, executive, and judicial branches of government. The legislative branch of government was separated into two houses with their own powers. Much more recently, the executive branch of government was separated in a substantial way by the twenty-fifth amendment. This addition to the Constitution allowed the vice president, under certain circumstances, to replace the president.

The judicial branch of government is the least representative of the will of the people. Supreme Court justices are not elected to office and have life terms. They often influence the affairs of the nation more than either the president or the Congress. The president and the Senate, through their powers to appoint and confirm judges, can enlarge the Supreme Court if it is thought necessary to counter any perceived abuse of judicial power.

In the executive branch of government, the president could be impeached and tried by the Congress, while laws passed by the Congress could face a presidential veto. A lesson on the system of checks and balances can be found in this book. The lesson goes into considerable detail on the subject.

Another concern over uncontrolled power was how to ensure that the military forces of the nation kept out of politics. One only has to think of Julius Caesar, Napoleon Bonaparte, and countless other generals who seized political power by overthrowing established governments using the force of arms. To make it clear that there would be civilian control over the armed forces, Article II, Section 2 made the President the commander in chief of the army and navy of the United States.

One way the writers of the Constitution tried to regulate and control power and enhance the system of checks and balances was to establish different kinds of power. There are four major types of power either found in the Constitution or derived from it. *Delegated or expressed powers* are those listed in the Constitution, such as the power of Congress to declare war. *Implied powers* are those reasonably suggested by the Constitution. For instance, the fact that the Congress is granted the power to coin money suggests that it is also reasonable for the Congress to authorize the printing of paper currency. *Concurrent powers* are powers common to the central government and the state governments. Both levels of government have the power to collect taxes, for example. *Reserved powers* are those that the Constitution neither gives to the central government nor forbids to the states. These powers belong to the people or to the states.

It is obvious that the writers of the Constitution, while desiring a fairly powerful central government, didn't want that government to have a monopoly of political power.

WHAT REQUIREMENTS SHOULD BE ESTABLISHED FOR HOLDING POWERFUL POSITIONS IN THE GOVERNMENT?

The Constitution was written in the closing years of the eighteenth century. Biases, prejudices, and feelings of nationalism and xenophobia, or the fear and dislike of foreigners, often came into play in the establishment of requirements for such officers of the government as representatives, senators, and presidents. A touch of gerontocracy, rule by elders, can be inferred by examining age requirements laid down in the Constitution. A representative had to be twenty-five years of age or more, a senator thirty years of age or older, and a president thirty-five years of age or older. This arrangement seems to make the length of life experiences a key factor in a politician's performance of his or her duties of office. The more responsibility connected with a political office, the more life experience was necessary, according to the writers of the Constitution.

Another factor that one sees in the requirements for several positions of power in the government is the length of time a potential candidate for office has been a citizen. Some critics of the Constitution claim that nationalism and xenophobia were at work in the requirement that a representative have been a citizen of the nation for at least seven years and a senator for at least nine years. The president must be a natural born (native born) citizen of the nation and have resided in the United States for at least fourteen years.

One counter argument to these views is that it seems logical that a representative or senator should have had some experience living in the nation for which he or she will be making laws affecting the lives of the American people. It can also be argued that a president was born in a foreign country might have dual loyalties which could interfere in doing what's best for American foreign affairs.

HOW CAN POWER BE OBTAINED, TAKEN AWAY AND TRANSFERRED PEACEFULLY?

In order to ensure that power would not become entrenched in one person or one group in the government, the writers of the Constitution established ways in which power could be legally obtained, taken away, and transferred from both individuals and groups.

In world history, power has often been obtained, taken away, or transferred by force or the threat of force. Conquering generals would establish dynasties. In some cases, power was literally purchased by men of wealth. Some Roman emperors obtained their thrones because they were the highest bidders.

The Constitution embodies the view that power should be obtained peacefully, either directly or indirectly by a vote of the citizens of the states or their elected representatives. Through the election process and through amendments to the Constitution, the problem of how power could be obtained, taken away, and transferred was answered.

Examples from the Constitution of power gains and losses:

- Article I, Section 2—Members of the House of Representatives have to face an election every two years. Winning an election will give a person power, but losing the election will see that power transferred to another representative.

- Article I, Section 2—The governor of the state calls special elections to fill vacancies in the state's representation. This is a way to peacefully transfer power.

- Article I, Section 2—The House of Representatives alone has the power to impeach (accuse) a government official of a crime. This is the first step in a process of taking away power from officials.

- Article I, Section 3—Senators must face election at the end of their six-year term, allowing again for a peaceful transfer of power.

- Article I, Section 3—The Senate tries all impeachment cases. A two-thirds majority vote is necessary for convictions. The chief justice of the Supreme Court must preside at the Senate trial of an impeached president.

- Article I, Section 5—Each house of Congress may expel members by a two-thirds vote. This is a good example of how power can be taken away.

- Article II, Section 1—The president faces the election process after his or her four-year term closes.

- Article II, Section 4—The president and all other civil officers of the United States may be removed from office if convicted of treason, bribery, or other high crimes. This provision protects civil officers from having their power taken away on minor charges.

- Article V—The process whereby the Constitution can be changed is spelled out in this article. Amendments have helped individuals and groups obtain power, lose power, and transfer power to other individuals and groups. Examples will follow showing how power relationships have changed over time.

- Amendment 15 (1870)—It states that neither the United States nor any state government can deny a citizen the right to vote because of race or color, or because the person was formerly a slave. This is the first time the Constitution addressed the voting qualifications. This amendment allowed former male slaves to vote, but not former female slaves. The central government failed to properly enforce the provisions of this amendment, and some states effectively denied the right of former male slaves to vote.

- Amendment 17 (1913)—This law stated that senators are to be elected directly by a vote of the people rather than by state legislatures. The people gained power, while state legislatures had power taken away.

- Amendment 19 (1920)—This law gave women the right to vote. In the United States, women reformers organized a women's rights convention at Seneca Falls, New York in 1848. Voting rights were discussed, and the movement spread. The movement was momentarily set aside during the Civil War (1861–1865). Women activists from both the North and the South turned their attention to the support of their respective sides in the war. After the war, women reformers were angered to see that the fifteenth amendment essentially gave the vote to males who had been slaves while women remained disenfranchised. (The original Constitution didn't mention voting qualifications. It was left up to each state to determine its own qualifications. The central government got involved when pressure from state governments demanded enfranchisement of certain groups nationwide in 1870). From 1878 to 1920, a proposed amendment to give women the right to vote was introduced to the Congress each year. After seventy-two years, the women's movement achieved its goal. Human groups that possess power generally are reluctant to share it.

- Amendment 20 (1933)—This amendment stipulates several provisions. If a president-elect dies before taking office, the vice president elect will become president. If a president-elect is disqualified, the vice president elect will serve as president until the president-elect qualifies. Congress may declare who will serve as president if neither the president-elect nor the vice president elect qualifies. All of these provisions are examples of how to arrange a peaceful transfer of power under unusual circumstances.

- Amendment 22 (1951)—This law limits the president to two terms of office. Power was taken away from the president so that a chief executive would not become overly entrenched in power, which can lead to abuses.

- Amendment 23 (1961)—The residents of the District of Columbia, which is not a state, are allowed to vote for presidents and vice presidents. Historically, the electorate has been broadened over the years, increasing the participation of people in decision-making.

- Amendment 24 (1964)—Poll taxes were abolished, thereby allowing many poor and minority citizens to vote in states that had imposed such taxes.

- Amendment 25 (1967)—This amendment has several provisions. The vice president becomes president if the president dies or must leave office. If the office of vice president is vacant, the president shall appoint and the Congress approve a new vice president. If the president declares himself or herself unable to continue as president, the vice president becomes acting president. Whenever the vice president and a majority of other officers declare that the president is disabled, the vice president becomes acting president. When the president declares that he or she is again able, he or she resumes presidential duties. But if the vice president and other officers disagree, Congress decides whether or not the president is able to resume the powers and duties of the office.

This amendment is an excellent example of how power can be taken away, obtained, and transferred not just once but several times if deemed necessary.

- Amendment 26 (1971)—This law gives eighteen-year-olds the right to vote. At the time of this writing, this was the most current expansion of the phrase, "We the people …".

Since 1788, when the Constitution went into effect, many new centers of power have entered American political life. While not mentioned in the Constitution, these new power centers have had a tremendous influence on the decision-making process by officials of the national government.

FOUR NEW POWER CENTERS:

- *Political Parties.* While there are no legal restrictions on the number of political parties that can be established, two of them dominate the nation's politics: the Democratic and Republican parties.

  These two parties can be quite dictatorial in forcing their members to vote a certain way on major issues. Each house of Congress makes its own rules, and one of these rules is that committee heads are appointed by the majority party in each house. Some political observers have said that the government of the United States is run by committees. If a committee rejects a bill, it doesn't come up for a vote by house members. This system does not encourage independent thought and action, but I can't think of any democratic nation where people haven't organized political parties to reach common goals of their members.

- *Special Interest Groups/Pressure Groups/Lobbyists.* Special interest groups are groups with a cause who want to influence lawmakers. Industries, large corporations, agricultural businesses, social organizations—the list of special interest groups could fill pages. The campaign contributions made by these groups have been seductive to many officers in the government.

- *Advanced Technology.* The impact of advanced technology on American political life has been developing rapidly. The Internet has been used to solicit campaign contributions from many thousands of people. Electronic voting is being tried out, and technical improvements in the mass media bring political events into the nation's homes. The danger lies in the fact that those who control the mass media are in a position to shape public opinion both for and against the policies and programs put forth by political leaders. Public opinion polls are used to advance and also to discredit selected candidates.

Consolidation of the mass media presents a challenge to those who feel that power should be controlled, separated, and balanced.

- *President's Cabinet.* You won't find it mentioned in the Constitution, but the development of the president's cabinet gives the president an important group of advisors who help him or her make political decisions. Cabinet members are heads of the executive departments of government.

As time goes by, there will undoubtedly emerge new centers of political power. There will be new power relationships, but eternal watchfulness will be necessary to preserve our democratic system.

A democratic nation is one in which, theoretically, the people rule. The word democracy comes from the Greek demos (common people) and kratos (rule). For the people to keep their power to rule, there are several necessities. I would put two at the top of my list. One is the need for people to use their skills in critical thinking to avoid gullibility. The other is the need for people to participate in the political process, especially by casting a thoughtful vote. Hopefully, when people vote they will carefully study the candidates for public offices as well as ballot measures. This is an ideal not to be taken lightly for a democratic society.

Title:	THE SOURCES OF SOME OF THE GREAT IDEAS UNDERLYING THE CONSTITUTION
Subject Area(s):	US history, civics
Skills:	Charting, analyzing, cause and effect relationships
Completion Time:	One standard period
Objective:	For students to recognize cause and effect relationships
Comments:	The teacher might hand out copies of the chart for this lesson and have the students carefully copy it.

A class discussion of the chart would be helpful for the students in preparing themselves for the quiz. Materials: ruler, pencil, pen, paper.

References:	Encyclopedias
Extension Activities:	Students could make brief research reports on the persons listed in the chart.

THE SOURCES OF SOME OF THE GREAT IDEAS UNDERLYING THE CONSTITUTION

Source	Time Period	Key Ideas
Aristotle (Greek philosopher)	4th century BC	• Governments must operate under a higher law than themselves • Citizens should participate in making laws that they are expected to obey
Jean Bodin (French philosopher)	16th century AD	• Individuals have a natural right to private property • Taxes should not be imposed upon citizens without their consent • Kings should be subject to fundamental constitutional laws
James Harrington (English political philosopher)	17th century AD	• A written constitution is essential if a nation is to achieve a high level of development • Good practices: a two-house legislature, a secret ballot, an indirect election of a president Important work: *Commonwealth of Oceana*, 1656
John Locke (English political philosopher)	17th century AD	• Mankind has entered into a "compact" to protect natural rights • Government rests upon the consent of the governed • If government breaks its compact with the people, the people have a right to rebel Important work: *Two Treatises of Government*, 1690
Thomas Hobbes (English philosopher)	17th century AD	• Security for all can be achieved only by a compact among people in which they transfer their individual power to a strong central power • The central government has a right to rule only if it abides by the agreement to keep the peace

Montesquieu (French philosopher)	18th century AD	• Political liberty involves separating the legislative, executive, and judicial powers of government • Liberty and respect for properly constituted law can exist together Important work: *The Spirit of the Laws*, 1748
Jean-Jacques Rousseau (French political philosopher)	18th century AD	• All citizens should participate in legislation • The "general will" of the people should guide government Important work: *The Social Contract*, 1762

_____   1.   A Greek philosopher of the fourth century BC:
(a) Locke (b) Bodin (c) Aristotle (d) Rousseau

_____   2.   He wrote _Two Treatises of Government:_
(a) Bodin (b) Aristotle (c) Locke (d) Montesquieu

_____   3.   He wrote _Commonwealth of Oceana:_
(a) Harrington (b) Bodin (c) Locke (d) Aristotle

_____   4.   He felt that mankind entered into a "compact" to protect natural rights:
(a) Bodin (b) Locke (c) Aristotle (d) Harrington

_____   5.   He was the author of _The Social Contract:_
(a) Bodin (b) Locke (c) Hobbes (d) Rousseau

_____   6.   He felt that all citizens should participate in legislation:
(a) Locke (b) Montesquieu (c) Bodin (d) Hobbes

_____   7.   He stated that all individuals should have a right to private property:
(a) Bodin (b) Harrington (c) Rousseau (d) Montesquieu

_____   8.   He proposed such ideas as a secret ballot and a two-house legislature:
(a) Hobbes (b) Locke (c) Harrington (d) Bodin

_____   9.   He wrote _The Spirit of the Laws:_
(a) Locke (b) Harrington (c) Bodin (d) Montesquieu

_____   10. He said that the "general will" of the people should guide government:
(a) Rousseau (b) Montesquieu (c) Hobbes (d) Locke

_____   11. This Greek philosopher thought that governments must operate under a higher law than themselves:
(a) Hobbes (b) Aristotle (c) Rousseau (d) Harrington

_____   12. This sixteenth- century French philosopher felt that kings should be subject to fundamental constitutional laws:
(a) Bodin (b) Hobbes (c) Locke (d) Montesquieu

_____   13. He said that liberty and respect for properly constituted law can exist together:
(a) Bodin (b) Locke (c) Montesquieu (d) Rousseau

_____   14. He said that the central government has a right to rule only if it abides by the agreement to keep the peace:
(a) Bodin (b) Hobbes (c) Rousseau (d) Harrington

_____   15. He said that the people have a right to rebel if government breaks its compact with the people:
(a) Rousseau (b) Montesquieu (c) Hobbes (d) Locke

_____   16. He argued that taxes should not be imposed upon citizens without their consent:
(a) Bodin (b) Rousseau (c) Montesquieu (d) Locke

_____   17. He advocated the indirect election of a president:
(a) Hobbes (b) Harrington (c) Locke (d) Bodin

_____   18. He said that a written constitution is essential if a nation is to achieve a high level of development:
(a) Aristotle (b) Harrington (c) Hobbes (d) Locke

_____   19. He said that political liberty involves separating the legislative, executive, and judicial powers of government:
(a) Hobbes (b) Locke (c) Montesquieu (d) Harrington

_____ 20. He felt that security for all could be achieved only by a compact among people in which they transferred their individual power to a strong central government:
(a) Locke (b) Hobbes (c) Montesquieu (d) Bodin

QUIZ ANSWERS—Lesson 1

__C__   1.   A Greek philosopher of the fourth century BC:
(a) Locke (b) Bodin (c) Aristotle (d) Rousseau

__C__   2.   He wrote *Two Treatises of Government*:
(a) Bodin (b) Aristotle (c) Locke (d) Montesquieu

__A__   3.   He wrote *Commonwealth of Oceana*:
(a) Harrington (b) Bodin (c) Locke (d) Aristotle

__B__   4.   He felt that mankind entered into a "compact" to protect natural rights:
(a) Bodin (b) Locke (c) Aristotle (d) Harrington

__D__   5.   He was the author of *The Social Contract*:
(a) Bodin (b) Locke (c) Hobbes (d) Rousseau

__B__   6.   He felt that all citizens should participate in legislation:
(a) Locke (b) Montesquieu (c) Bodin (d) Hobbes

__A__   7.   He stated that all individuals should have a right to private property:
(a) Bodin (b) Harrington (c) Rousseau (d) Montesquieu

__C__   8.   He proposed such ideas as a secret ballot and a two-house legislature:
(a) Hobbes (b) Locke (c) Harrington (d) Bodin

__D__   9.   He wrote *The Spirit of the Laws*:
(a) Locke (b) Harrington (c) Bodin (d) Montesquieu

__A__   10. He said that the "general will" of the people should guide government:
(a) Rousseau (b) Montesquieu (c) Hobbes (d) Locke

__B__   11. This Greek philosopher thought that governments must operate under a higher law than themselves:
(a) Hobbes (b) Aristotle (c) Rousseau (d) Harrington

__A__   12. This sixteenth-century French philosopher felt that kings should be subject to fundamental constitutional laws:
(a) Bodin (b) Hobbes (c) Locke (d) Montesquieu

__D__   13. He said that liberty and respect for properly constituted law can exist together:
(a) Bodin (b) Locke (c) Montesquieu (d) Rousseau

__C__   14. He said that the central government has a right to rule only if it abides by the agreement to keep the peace:
(a) Bodin (b) Hobbes (c) Rousseau (d) Harrington

__D__   15. He said that the people have a right to rebel if government breaks its compact with the people:
(a) Rousseau (b) Montesquieu (c) Hobbes (d) Locke

__A__   16. He argued that taxes should not be imposed upon citizens without their consent:
(a) Bodin (b) Rousseau (c) Montesquieu (d) Locke

__B__   17. He advocated the indirect election of a president:
(a) Hobbes (b) Harrington (c) Locke (d) Bodin

__B__   18. He said that a written constitution is essential if a nation is to achieve a high level of development:
(a) Aristotle (b) Harrington (c) Hobbes (d) Locke

__C__   19. He said that political liberty involves separating the legislative, executive, and judicial powers of government:
(a) Hobbes (b) Locke (c) Montesquieu (d) Harrington

__B__   20. He felt that security for all could be achieved only by a compact among people in which they transferred their individual power to a strong central government:
(a) Locke (b) Hobbes (c) Montesquieu (d) Bodin

Title:	HOW THE CONSTITUTION ALLOWS FOR CHANGE
Subject Area:	US history, civics
Skills:	Analyzing, using charts, conceptualizing
Completion Time:	One standard period plus assigned homework
Objective:	For students to analyze methods of change in society in general and in the Constitution specifically
Comments:	Students should have a class discussion on Chart A, CHART OF COMMON POINTS OF VIEW ON HOW A SOCIETY SHOULD BE CHANGED. Then students should review a copy of Chart B on the four ways of amending the Constitution in preparation for a quiz. A chart quiz form is included in this lesson.
Materials:	Charts, chart quiz forms, pen, pencil
References:	The Constitution of the United States
Extension Activities:	A class discussion might be held on the topic: Is American Society Changing Too Fast? This could also be an assigned essay.

Chart A

CHART OF COMMON POINTS OF VIEW ON HOW A SOCIETY SHOULD BE CHANGED

Points of view onchange	How much change should take place	The direction in which change should take place	How fast change should occur	What methods should be used to effect change
Radical	Complete or drastic change	Looks toward the future—stresses innovation, the new and untried	Immediately	Peaceful or violent as necessary
Liberal	Considerable	Looks to a better future through a reformation of the existing social system	Soon	Peaceful
Conservative	Little	Looks to the preservation of what is seen as the best of what currently exists	Very slowly and carefully	Peaceful
Reactionary	Complete or drastic change	Looks back to some given time in the past as a guide to the present and future	Immediately	Peaceful or violent as necessary

Student Handout—Lesson 2

QUIZ ON VIEWS ON HOW TO CHANGE SOCIETY

Directions: Place the appropriate letter or letters (a, b, c, or d) representing current views in the spaces provided.

Answer Key: <u>a</u>. Radical   <u>b</u>. Liberal   <u>c</u>. Conservative   <u>d</u>. Reactionary

_____   1. Calls for slow change.

_____   2. Two views that call for immediate change.

_____   3. These views allow for the use of violent methods when necessary.

_____   4. Focuses on the preservation of the society as it is.

_____   5. Calls for a considerable reformation of the existing society.

_____   6. Looks to the past as a guide.

_____   7. Stresses innovation, the new, and the untried.

_____   8. Two views that mostly represent peaceful ways of change.

_____   9. They look for drastic change to be made in society.

_____   10. This view is different from other views in its choice of the direction toward which change should take place.

Chart B

FOUR WAYS OF AMENDING THE CONSTITUTION

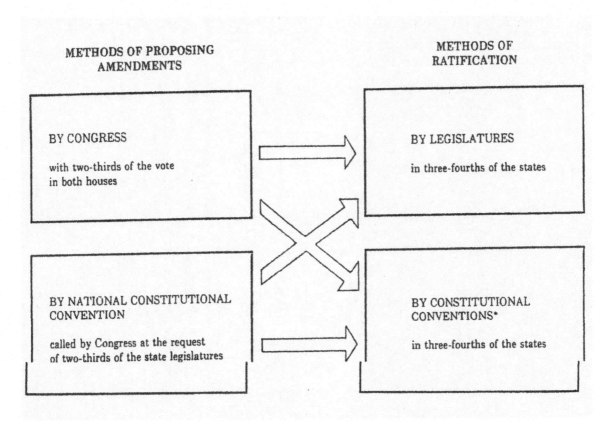

METHODS OF PROPOSING
AMENDMENTS

METHODS OF
RATIFICATION

BY CONGRESS

with two-thirds of the vote
in both houses

BY LEGISLATURES

in three-fourths of the states

BY NATIONAL CONSTITUTIONAL
CONVENTION

called by Congress at the request
of two-thirds of the state legislatures

BY CONSTITUTIONAL
CONVENTIONS*

in three-fourths of the states

*Amendment 21 was ratified by Constitutional Conventions

FOUR WAYS OF AMENDING THE CONSTITUTION

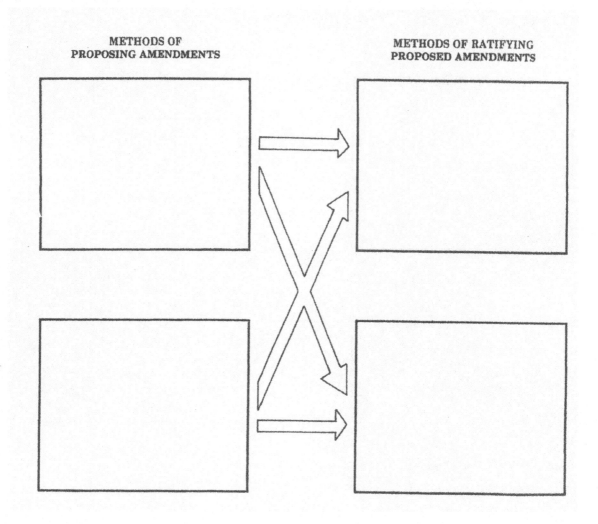

Quiz Answers — Lesson 2

QUIZ ON VIEWS ON HOW TO CHANGE SOCIETY

Directions: Place the appropriate letter or letters (a, b, c, or d) representing current views in the spaces provided.

Answer Key: a. Radical   b. Liberal   c. Conservative   d. Reactionary

C _____   1. Calls for slow change.

A,D _____   2. Two views that call for immediate change.

A,D _____   3. These views allow for the use of violent methods when necessary.

C _____   4. Focuses on the preservation of the society as it is.

B _____   5. Calls for a considerable reformation of the existing society.

D _____   6. Looks to the past as a guide.

A _____   7. Stresses innovation, the new and the untried.

B,C _____   8. Two views that mostly represent peaceful ways of change.

A,D _____   9. They look for drastic change to be made in society.

D _____   10. This view is different from other views in its choice of the direction toward which change should take place.

Title:	MATHEMATICS IN THE FABRIC OF THE CONSTITUTION OF THE UNITED STATES
Subject Area(s):	US history, civics
Skills:	Word recognition, scanning written material selectively
Completion Time:	One standard period
Objective:	For students to be able to locate specific information in an historical document
Comments:	Students could be given the answers to the first ten questions in the exercise and then continue on their own. They would have to fill in the twenty-five blanks left in the exercise. This would make it easy to assign percentage grades.
Materials:	Exercise sheets, pen, pencil
References:	The Constitution of the United States
Extension Activities:	Students could write an essay on the topic, "Why Is Mathematics So Important in Our Plan for Government?" (Example: fairness usually calls for a division of power.)

MATHEMATICS IN THE FABRIC OF THE CONSTITUTION OF THE UNITED STATES

Directions: Place the correct whole number or fraction of a number in the numbered blanks provided in this lesson.

Congress is divided into (1)_____parts. Representatives are chosen every (2)_____years. A representative must be at least (3)_____years old. A representative must have been a US citizen for (4)_____years. A census, or count of the people, must be taken every (5)_____years. Each state shall have at least (6)_____representative(s). The Senate of the United States shall be composed of (7)_____senators from each state. A senator's term of office is (8)_____years. In the Senate, each senator shall have (9)_____vote. Only (10)_____of the senators are elected in any one election year. A senator must be at least (11)_____years old. A senator must be a US citizen for at least (12)_____years to be eligible for election. To convict a government official, (13)_____of the senators present must vote guilty. Congress must meet at least (14)_____a year. Neither the House nor the Senate can hold meetings for business unless it has a quorum; that is, more than (15)_____the members must be present. In either the House or the Senate, (16)_____of the members must agree if they wish to expel a member. If (17)_____of the members of either house favor it, the Congressional Record must show how each member voted on any question. The president can veto a bill, but a (18)_____majority of both houses overrides the veto. The president serves a (19)_____year term of office. To become president, a person must be at least (20)_____years old. To become president, a person must have lived in the United States for (21)_____years. A president can make a treaty, but (22)_____of the senators present must approve it. To convict a person of treason, at least (23)_____witnesses must testify in court that the accused person committed the same act of treason. Amendments can be proposed by a (24)_____vote of both the Senate and the House or by the legislature of (25)_____of the states. An amendment is ratified by being approved by a (26)_____vote of all state legislatures or by conventions in (27)_____of the states. Government under the Constitution could begin after (28)_____states approved it at special conventions. In many disputes that involve more than (29)_____dollars, either side in the dispute can insist in having a jury trial or both can agree not to have a jury. No person can have more than (30)_____terms as president. If the vice president and a majority of the Cabinet or some other group do not agree that the president has recovered, they must notify Congress before (31)_____days have passed. Congress must meet within (32)_____hours. They have (33)_____days to discuss the issue. If (34)_____or more of each house votes against the president, the vice president continues to serve as acting president. Citizens can vote when they reach the age of (35)_____.

ANSWER SHEET FOR MATHEMATICS IN THE FABRIC
OF THE CONSTITUTION OF THE UNITED STATES

Question No.	Answer	Article No.	Section No.	Clause No.
1	Two	I	1	
2	Two	I	2	1
3	Twenty-five	I	2	2
4	Seven	I	2	2
5	Ten	I	2	3
6	One	I	2	3
7	Two	I	3	1
8	Six	I	3	1
9	One	I	3	1
10	One-third	I	3	2
11	Thirty	I	3	3
12	Nine	I	3	3
13	Two-thirds	I	3	6
14	Once	I	4	2
15	Half	I	5	1
16	Two-thirds	I	5	2
17	One-fifth	I	5	3
18	Two-thirds	I	7	2
19	Four	II	1	1
20	Thirty-five	II	1	5
21	Fourteen	II	1	5
22	Two-thirds	II	2	2
23	Two	III	3	1
24	Two-thirds	V		
25	Two-thirds	V		
26	Three-fourths	V		
27	Three-fourths	V		
28	Nine	VII		
29	Twenty	Amendment #7		
30	Two	Amendment #22		

31		Four	Amendment #25		
32		Forty-eight	Amendment #25		
33		Twenty-one	Amendment #25		
34		Two-thirds	Amendment #25		
35		Two-thirds	Amendment #25		
36		Eighteen	Amendment #26		

Title:	INVESTIGATING THE CONSTITUTION
Subject Area(s):	US history, civics
Skills:	Research, analyzing
Completion Time:	One class period, plus homework
Objective:	For students to be able to search out topics in the Constitution
Comments:	Students might work in pairs in this lesson
References:	The Constitution
Extension Activities:	Students, in a brainstorming session, could think of more topics not in the list given to them

INVESTIGATING THE CONSTITUTION

Directions: Identify the article, section, and/or amendment associated with each of the following subjects:

1. Admission of new states

2. Advice and consent

3. Appointment of ambassadors

4. A quorum to do business

5. Assembly, Right of

6. Bill

7. Bill of Attainder

8. Bill of Rights

9. Bribery

10. Church and state

11. Citizenship

12. Civil Rights

13. Commander in chief

14. Commerce clause

15. Congress

16. Congressional Record

17. Corruption of blood

18. Counterfeiting

19. Court

20. Cruel and unusual punishments

21. Double jeopardy

INVESTIGATING THE CONSTITUTION

1. Admission of new states: Article IV, Section 3

2. Advice and consent: Article II, Section 2

3. Appointment of ambassadors: Article II, Section 2

4. A quorum to do business: Article I, Section 5

5. Assembly, Right of: Amendment I

6. Bill: Article I, Section 7

7. Bill of Attainder: Article I, Section 9

8. Bill of Rights: Amendments I to X

9. Bribery: Article II, Section 4

10. Church and state: Article VI, Amendment I

11. Citizenship: Amendment XIV

12. Civil Rights: Amendments XIV XV

13. Commander in chief: Article II, Section 2

14. Commerce clause: Article 1, Section 8

15. Congress: Article I, Amendment XII

16. Congressional Record: Article I, Section 5

17. Corruption of blood: Article III, Section 3

18. Counterfeiting: Article I, Section 8

19. Court: Article III

20. Cruel and unusual punishments: Amendment VIII

21. Double jeopardy: Amendment V

22. Due process of law: Amendments V and XIV

23. Elastic clause: Article I, Section 9

24. Electoral College: Article II, Section 1; Amendments XII and XXIII

25. Ex post facto: Article I, Section 9

26. Executive branch: Article II

27. Extradition: Article IV, Section 2

28. Freedom of religion: Amendment I

29. Freedom of speech: Amendment I

30. Freedom of the press: Amendment I

31. House of Representatives: Article I, Amendment XIII

32. Immunity, congressional: Article I, Section 6

33. Impeachment: Article I, Sections 2 and 3; Article II, Section 4

34. Income tax: Article I, Section 9; Amendment XVI

35. Judicial branch: Article III

36. Judicial review: Article III, Section 2

37. Jury and trial by jury: Article III, Section 2

38. Lame duck amendment: Amendment XX

39. Legislative branch: Article I

40. Letters of marque and reprisal: Article I, Section 8

41. Militia: Article I, Section 8; Amendments II and V

42. National debt: Article VI

43. Pardon: Article II, Section 2

44. Poll tax: Amendment XXIV

Title:	CONSTITUTIONAL DEBATE TOPICS
Subject Area(s):	Government, US history
Skills:	Debating, analyzing, synthesizing, researching
Completion Time:	To be determined by the teacher
Objective:	For students to debate constitutional issues
Comments:	You may wish to use one or more of the following debate forms in the assignment of debate topics to your students

1. The Cross-Examination Form (developed at the University of Oregon):

In this debate form, each speaker is cross-examined by an opposing speaker. Then each side presents a rebuttal. Most teams consist of two speakers. The debate is structured in this way:

First affirmative speaker (8 minutes)
  Cross-examined by second negative speaker (3 minutes)
  First negative speaker (8 minutes)
  Cross-examined by first affirmative speaker (3 minutes)
  Second affirmative speaker (8 minutes)
  Cross-examined by first negative speaker (3 minutes)
  Second negative speaker (8 minutes)
  Cross-examined by second affirmative speaker (3 minutes)

Rebuttal Speeches:

  First negative speaker (3 minutes)
  First affirmative speaker (3 minutes)
  Second negative speaker (3 minutes)
  Second affirmative speaker (3 minutes)

2. The Heckling Debate Form:

A type of formal debate, similar in some ways to the cross-examination form, designed to simulate legislative debate as practiced in the state legislatures or in the House of Representatives or the Senate. Speakers on both sides of the proposition can be questioned by members of the opposing teams, with limits set for the number of questions and the time in which they can be asked.

3. The Lincoln-Douglas Debate Form:

A two-person formal debate named in honor of the famous duo who used this form to debate the slavery issue in 1858 and 1859. Each speaker delivers a main speech and then is given time for a brief rebuttal speech.

4. The Direct Clash Debate Form:

A form of debate in which affirmative and negative proponents clash (stage verbally aggressive attacks on each other's statements) on specific issues in a proposition until one team wins three clashes, as decided by the judge, and is declared the winner. The judge may take an active role in this type of debate.

5. The Standard Debate Form:

This is one of the most popular and widely used debate forms in the United States. It is structured as follows:

First affirmative speaker (10 minutes)
First negative speaker (10 minutes)
Second affirmative speaker (10 minutes)
Second negative speaker (10 minutes)

First negative rebuttal (5 minutes)
First affirmative rebuttal (5 minutes)
Second negative rebuttal (5 minutes)
Second affirmative rebuttal (5 minutes)

Materials: Debate preparation forms, pen, paper

References: Recently proposed amendments, books on the Constitution

Extension Activities: Students could represent state legislatures and vote on proposed amendments to the Constitution after classroom debates and class discussions

Student Handout—Lesson 5

CONSTITUTIONAL DEBATE TOPICS, DEBATE PREPARATION FORM

Definitions of debating terms:

Debate: A formal, oral confrontation between two individuals, teams, or groups who present arguments to support opposing sides of a proposition, generally according to a set form or procedure.

Proposition: The statement upon which the debate is based.

Affirmative: Arguing in favor of a proposition.

Negative: Arguing against a proposition.

Rebuttal: The response to your opponents' arguments and counter-arguments.

DEBATE PREPARATION FORM:

Directions: Write two forms, one for the affirmative side of the proposition selected by you or assigned to you and one for the negative side of the proposition.

1. State exactly what you're trying to prove.

2. State briefly your best argument in support of your position.

3. State briefly your second-best argument in support of your position.

4. State briefly your third-best argument in support of your position.

5. State briefly what you think your opponent will be trying to prove.

6. State briefly what you think your opponent's best argument in support of his or her position will be.

7. State briefly what you think your opponent's second-best argument in support of his or her position will be.

8. State briefly what you think your opponent's third-best argument will be.

9. How would you argue against each of your opponent's best arguments?
   (A)
   (B)
   (C)

CONSTITUTIONAL DEBATE TOPICS

Resolutions based on statements in the preamble:

Resolved: That the blessings of liberty have not been secured for all Americans.

Resolved: That justice has not been established in the United States.

Resolutions based on statements in Article I:

Resolved: That the age requirement to be a representative be lowered to twenty-one.

Resolved: That the two-year term of office for a representative be extended to four years.

Resolved: That there should be a limit of two terms for a representative.

Resolved: That the age requirement to be a senator be lowered to twenty-five.

Resolved: That the Congress should share the power with the president in the declaration of war.

Resolutions based on statements in Article II:

Resolved: That the age requirement to be president be lowered to thirty.

Resolved: That the presidential term of office be extended to six years.

Resolved: That the president be elected by a popular vote of the people.

Resolved: That treaties be approved by a majority of the senators.

Resolved: That the unconditional power of the president to grant reprieves and pardons be abolished.

Resolved: That members of the president's cabinet be elected by a popular vote of the people.

Resolutions based on statements in Article III:

Resolved: That Supreme Court justices be elected by a popular vote of the people.

Resolved: That the term of office for a justice of the Supreme Court be six years.

Resolutions based on statements in Article IV:

Resolved: That states be allowed to secede from the Union.

Resolutions based on statements in Article V:

Resolved: That amendments to the Constitution be ratified by a majority of the state legislatures.

Resolutions based on statements in Article VI:

Resolved: That the Constitution be amended to allow laws of international organizations in which the United States holds membership to supersede the supremacy of the Constitution.

Resolutions dealing with various proposed amendments to the Constitution:

Resolved: That capital punishment be made illegal in the United States.

Resolved: That the right to work be added to the Constitution.

Resolved: That the right to bear arms be restricted by a constitutional amendment.

Resolved: That the burning of the flag of the United States be made illegal.

Resolved: That abortions, except in cases of rape, incest, or danger to the mother, be made illegal in the United States.

Resolved: That prayers be approved in public schools.

Resolved: That English be made the official language of the United States.

Resolved: That equal rights for women be secured by an amendment to the Constitution.

Resolved: That the voting age in federal elections be lowered to sixteen.

Resolved: That the income tax be abolished and replaced by a national sales tax.

Title:	THE SYSTEM OF CHECKS AND BALANCES
Subject Area:	Civics
Skills:	Analyzing, identifying pertinent data
Completion Time:	One standard period plus homework
Objective:	For students to understand the system of checks and balances
Comments:	Students should have a discussion of the meaning of power. Power is a dangerous thing when it is concentrated in a few hands. The system of checks and balances was instituted to keep power separated in our national government.
Materials:	Pen, paper, The System of Checks and Balances Chart
References:	Textbooks in government
Extension Activities:	Students could consider whether or not there is a real balance of power among the three branches of our national government. New checks and balances might be discussed and considered.

THE SYSTEM OF CHECKS AND BALANCES

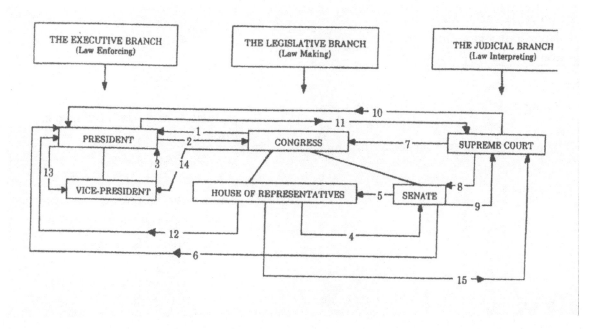

ASSIGNMENT:

Starting from #1 in the chart shown above, list all of the checks and balances you can find in either the Constitution or in the right of "judicial review." The right of judicial review was developed by John Marshall, the third Chief Justice of the US Supreme Court. His argument that the right to determine when the limits of the constitution have been violated lies with the Supreme Court has become an American legal tradition.

When you find a check in the Constitution, cite the article, section, or amendment that applies. In the case of Supreme Court power to determine a law's constitutionality, the term "judicial review" will be sufficient.
(This caption was placed below the picture in the original.)

Exercise Answers—Lesson 6

KEY TO THE LESSON ON THE SYSTEM OF CHECKS AND BALANCES

Governmental entity that uses its power in order to keep a balance of power among the three branches of government	Power of a governmental entity being checked	Example
1. Congress	President	Article I, Section 7 Congress may pass a bill into law over the President's veto
2. President	Congress	Article I, Section 7 A presidential veto returns a bill to the Congress unsigned into law
3. Vice president	President	Amendment 25, Section 4 Whenever the vice president and a majority of other officers decide that the president is disabled, the vice president becomes acting president
4. House of Representatives	Senate	Article I, Section 7 All bills for raising revenue must originate in the House
5. Senate	House of Representatives	Article I, Section 3 The Senate has the sole power to try impeachment
6. Senate	President	Article II, Section 2 The president may make treaties, but they must be approved by a two-thirds vote of the Senate
7. Supreme Court	Congress	It's not a part of the Constitution, but the Supreme Court has established its power to declare acts of Congress unconstitutional

8. Supreme Court	Senate	Article I, Section 3 When the President is being tried by the Senate in an impeachment case, the Chief Justice of the Supreme Court must preside
9. Senate	Supreme Court	Article II, Section 2 The Senate has the power to approve the presidential appointments, including the addition of judges to the Supreme Court
10. Supreme Court	President	The Supreme Court may declare executive actions not constitutional
11. President	Supreme Court	Article II, Section 2 The president can appoint judges to the Supreme Court with the advice and consent of the Senate
12. House of Representatives	President	Article I, Section 2 The House has the sole power of impeachment (the right to accuse a government official of a crime)
13. President	Vice president	Amendment 25, Section 4 After the vice president has become acting president, the president can resume his powers and displace the acting president with a written declaration sent to president pro tempore of the Senate and to the Speaker of the House
14. Congress	Vice president	Amendment 25, Section 4 The Congress decides if the President or the Vice President shall keep the power of the "oval office" when conflicting claims to the presidential position occur

15. House of Representatives	Supreme Court	Article I, Section 2 The House has the sole power of impeachment of government officials

Title:	OUTLINE FOR A REPORT ON AN AMENDMENT TO THE CONSTITUTION OF THE UNITED STATES
Subject Area:	Civics
Skills:	Analyzing, library research
Completion Time:	One standard period plus homework
Objective:	For students to understand the concept of change in the operation of a government
Comments:	Students should read over the amendments to the Constitution, paying attention to the reason(s) why each amendment was proposed and ratified.
Materials:	Pen, paper, report outline
References:	Encyclopedias, textbooks in government
Extension Activities:	Students could list amendments that they would like to see in the Constitution. A master list could then be written on the blackboard for students to discuss. Each amendment would have to pass a two-thirds vote of the class to be approved.

OUTLINE FOR A REPORT ON AN AMENDMENT TO THE CONSTITUTION OF THE UNITED STATES

1. Number of the amendment:

2. Year ratified:

3. Main points of the amendment:

4. Historical importance of the amendment:

5. Your personal reaction to the amendment:

6. Source(s) of information:

Title:	A STATE OF THE UNION ADDRESS
Subject Area(s):	US history, civics
Skills:	Locating information, using original source material, analyzing
Completion Time:	One standard period
Objective:	For students to use original source material to support or refute a given statement.
Comments:	Students should be specific in their answers. In most cases, citing an Article will not suffice.
Materials:	Constitution Exercise "Prove It," pen, pencil
References:	The Constitution of the United States
Extension Activities:	Students could make up five statements, either correct or incorrect, based on the Constitution.

CONSTITUTION EXERCISE: "PROVE IT"

Find the appropriate article, section, and/or amendment in the Constitution to prove these statements either correct or incorrect. Write "correct" or "incorrect" first and then your proof.

1. Gilda was told she could not vote because of her sex.
2. Joe Corrupt said that as a Senator he deserved three votes.
3. The Chief Justice said that he presides over the Senate when the President is impeached.
4. A man with green hair was told he could not vote.
5. Hey, I think it is against the federal law to drink alcoholic beverages.
6. If the President is gravely ill, there's nothing that can be done.
7. Herbert, can the government borrow money?
8. "We'll lower your salary, Mr. President," threatened the senator.
9. Southern California' wants to make itself an independent state, if the California state legislature approves.
10. The judge told the accused he had to confess to the crime before the jury.
11. Congress shall make him a prince.
12. For that rat, bail is $4,000,000.
13. A Nevadan wants to run for the Senate in Utah.
14. The ERA would have become the twenty-seventh amendment if thirty state legislatures had approved it.
15. H.R. 1473, a bill to draft women, reaches the president's desk on Feb. 1. The President reads it on Feb. 24 and vetoes it.
16. Charlie Cheap says that the government cannot collect taxes from him.
17. The US Supreme Court approves the president's appointment of his nephew, Sheldon P. Nerd, to the 4th Circuit Court of Appeals.
18. The President prepares a treaty with Iran which pledges our help if Russia violates Iranian borders. Of the ninety-one senators present, fifty-one vote approval of the treaty and it passes.
19. The vice president was surprised. Forty-three senators voted yes on a bill; forty-three voted no. He said, "I'll break the tie!"
20. The judge condemned Laslo Bunkerson to death by being dunked in acid. Death would be horrible for the convicted hatchet slayer of three children.
21.

CONSTITUTION EXERCISE: "PROVE IT"

1.	Incorrect	Amendment XIX, Sec. 1
2.	Incorrect	Article I, Sec. 3 ; Amend. XVII
3.	Correct	Article I, Sec. 3
4.	Incorrect	Amendment XV, Sec. 1
5.	Incorrect	Amendment XXI (Correct: Amendment XVIII)
6.	Incorrect	Amendment XXV, Sec. 4; Article II, Sec. 1
7.	Correct	Amendment I, Sec. 8(b)
8.	Incorrect	Article II, Sec. 1(g)
9.	Incorrect	Article IV, Sec. 3(a)
10.	Incorrect	Amendment V
11.	Incorrect	Article I, Sec. 9(g)
12.	Incorrect	Amendment VIII
13.	Incorrect	Article I, Sec. 3
14.	Incorrect	Article V
15.	Incorrect	Article I, Sec. 7
16.	Incorrect	Article I, Sec. 8; Amendment XVI
17.	Incorrect	Article II, Sec. 2(b)
18.	Incorrect	Article II, Sec. 2(b)
19.	Correct	Article I, Sec. 2
20.	Incorrect	Amendment VIII

Teacher Instructions—Lesson 10

Title:	ISMS, CRACIES, AND ARCHIES IN THE CONSTITUTION
Subject Area(s):	US history, civics
Skills:	Analyzing; differentiating among fact, inference and opinion; using primary source material
Completion Time:	One standard period plus homework
Objective:	For students to locate evidence for statements they make
Comments:	Since the pronoun "he" used in the Constitution could arguably have been used to include both sexes, it is difficult to find sex discrimination in the Constitution. The Constitution does not mention black people specifically, so albocracy—domination by white people—is difficult to establish by referring to the Constitution.
Materials:	Student sheets, pen, pencil
References:	The Constitution of the United States
Extension Activities:	Students could recommend the inclusion in the Constitution of any political idea from the listing that is not currently a part of the Constitution.

ISMS, CRACIES, AND ARCHIES IN THE CONSTITUTION

Directions:
(1) Examine the given listing of selected political ideas.
(2) Try to find influences on the Constitution of as many of the ideas from the listing shown below as you can. Cite the specific Article, Section, and Amendment that will support your choices.

Example: 1. Term: gerontocracy

A. Statement: The relationship of age to increased responsibility is built into the Constitution.

B. Evidence:

Article I, Section 2—There is a requirement that representatives be at least twenty-five years of age.

Article I, Section 3—There is a requirement that senators be at least thirty years of age.

Article II, Section 1—There is a requirement that a president be at least thirty-five years of age.

SELECTED LISTING OF POLITICAL IDEAS

1. albocracy—the domination of the government by white people
2. anarchism—government is evil and unnecessary
3. andocracy—domination by men
4. aristocracy—rule by people of highest social status
5. authoritarianism—absolute obedience to authority
6. autocracy—rule by one person whose powers are not openly disputed
7. bureaucracy—administration of a government by bureaus staffed with nonelected officials
8. communism—everyone works according to his ability and receives according to his need
9. democracy—a system in which the governed have the right to choose their political leaders
10. fascism—a dictatorship of the extreme right, typically through the merging of state and business leadership, with an ideology of belligerent nationalism
11. federalism—a union of states recognizing the sovereignty of a central authority while retaining certain residual powers of government
12. gerontocracy—domination by elderly people in society
13. gynecocracy—domination of the government by women
14. kakistocracy — domination of the government by the worst elements of society
15. materialism—all goals in life are material; spiritual aspects of life are not recognized
16. monarchy—rule by a hereditary chieftain
17. oligarchy—domination of the government by a small clique
18. pedantocracy—rule by theorists with little practical experience
19. plutocracy—rule by the wealthy

20. protocracy (meritocracy)—rule by the most competent, active, and alert members of society
21. romanticism—the heart and the emotions are more important than reason
22. social darwinism—only the fit should survive... let the poor die!
23. socialism—collective ownership of all productive property and natural resources
24. technocracy—rule by scientists, engineers, and technicians
25. thalassocracy—a government based on sea power
26. theocracy—domination of a government by clergymen
27. timocracy—a state governed by the principles of honor and military glory

Exercise: (follow the form of the example given for this lesson)
  1. Term:

A. Statement

B. Evidence:

  2. Term:

A. Statement

B. Evidence:

Title:	SOME IMPORTANT DELEGATES AT THE CONSTITUTIONAL CONVENTION (PHILADELPHIA—1787)
Subject Area(s):	US history, civics
Skills:	Chart comprehension
Completion Time:	One standard period for class discussion plus homework
Objective:	For students to recognize the importance of strong personalities in the making of the historical record.
Comments:	Class discussion of the chart "Some Important Delegates at the Constitutional Convention (Philadelphia–1787)" is recommended before the quiz for this lesson is given.
Materials:	Charts, quiz papers, pen, pencil
References:	Textbooks on the history of the Constitution of the United States.
Extension Activities:	Students could do brief biographical sketches on the delegates at the Constitutional Convention.

SOME IMPORTANT DELEGATES AT THE CONSTITUTIONAL CONVENTION
(PHILADELPHIA–1787)

Delegate	State Represented	Contributions to the Effort to Create a Constitution
Oliver Ellsworth	Connecticut	A great lawyer of the day whose knowledge of government questions was most helpful at the convention
Benjamin Franklin	Pennsylvania	A master of the art of of compromise; his good humor cooled off many an angry delegate
Elbridge Gerry	Massachusetts	As a merchant, he wanted commerce regulated by a strong central government
Alexander Hamilton	New York	A major advocate for a strong authoritarian central government, he worked hard for the ratification of the constitution in New York
William Samuel Johnson	Connecticut	Having a Doctor of Laws degree from Oxford helped him to make a considerable contribution to the legal work involved in developing the Constitution
Rufus King	Massachusetts	He sided strongly with James Madison
James Madison	Virginia	Called the "Father of the Constitution," he authored the Virginia Plan, or large-state plan, that would have given most of the legislative power to states with large populations; developed a system of checks and balances to keep power separated among the legislative, executive, and judicial branches of the government; and tried to balance state and federal government powers
George Mason	Virginia	He wanted a Bill of Rights
Governeur Morris	Pennsylvania	He was chairman of the convention committee on style, and he was responsible for the wording of the Constitution
Robert Morris	Pennsylvania	He nominated George Washington as presiding officer of the convention; as a businessman, he wanted a strong central government with the power to tax
William Paterson	New Jersey	He advocated the small-state plan, which would have given all states equal representation in the congress

Edmund Randolf	Virginia	He presented James Madison's Virginia Plan (large-state plan) to the convention
Roger Sherman	Connecticut	He worked hard for ratification of the Constitutionand came up with the great compromise: a two- house legislature with large states favored in one house and all states with equal voting power in the other house
George Washington	Virginia	The presiding officer of the Constitutional Convention, he was the most popular political leader in the thirteen states
James Wilson	Pennsylvania	He helped to frame the judicial clauses in the Constitution, and he presented a plan for choosing the president that was written into the Constitution
George Wyth	Virginia	The law teacher of John Marshall, James Madison, and Thomas Jefferson, he fought for ratification of the Constitution in Virginia

CONSTITUTIONAL DELEGATE QUIZ

_____ 1. He represented Pennsylvania at the Constitutional Convention:
(a) Alexander Hamilton (b) Benjamin Franklin (c) James Madison (d) Oliver Ellsworth

_____ 2. James Madison was a delegate from:
(a) New York (b) Massachusetts (c) Connecticut (d) Virginia

_____ 3. New York sent this man to the Constitutional Convention:
(a) Alexander Hamilton (b) James Madison (c) Elbridge Gerry (d) James Wilson

_____ 4. George Washington was from this state:
(a) New York (b) Massachusetts (c) Virginia (d) New Jersey

_____ 5. William Paterson represented this state:
(a) New Jersey (b) Pennsylvania (c) Massachusetts (d) Virginia

_____ 6. He presided over the Constitutional Convention:
(a) Benjamin Franklin (b) George Washington (c) James Madison (d) Alexander Hamilton

_____ 7. He presented James Madison's Virginia Plan to the Constitutional Convention:
(a) Thomas Jefferson (b) Edmund Randolf (c) George Washington (d) William Patterson

_____ 8. The small-state plan was supported by:
(a) James Madison (b) Benjamin Franklin (c) Alexander Hamilton (d) William Patterson

_____ 9. George Mason is known for his advocacy of:
(a) the large-state plan (b) the small-state plan (c) a Bill of Rights (d) a return to the Articles of Confederation

_____ 10. He is called the "Father of the Constitution":
(a) George Washington (b) James Madison (c) Benjamin Franklin (d) Alexander Hamilton

_____ 11. He was the law teacher of John Marshall, James Madison, and Thomas Jefferson:
(a) James Wilson (b) Roger Sherman (c) George Wyth (d) Edmund Randolf

_____ 12. He was a big businessman who wanted a strong central government with the power to tax:
(a) Robert Morris (b) George Mason (c) William Paterson (d) William Samuel Johnson

_____ 13. He is credited with coming up with the Great Compromise, a two-house legislature:
(a) William Paterson (b) James Madison (c) Roger Sherman (d) Alexander Hamilton

_____ 14. He held a Doctor of Laws degree from Oxford University:
(a) Alexander Hamilton (b) Benjamin Franklin (c) James Madison (d) William Samuel Johnson

_____ 15. As a merchant, he wanted commerce regulated by a strong central government:
(a) Oliver Ellsworth (b) Elbridge Gerry (c) James Madison (d) Benjamin Franklin

_____ 16. His good humor cooled off many an angry delegate:
(a) George Washington (b) Benjamin Franklin (c) Alexander Hamilton (d) Oliver Ellsworth

_____ 17. He advocated a strong, authoritarian central government and fought hard for the ratification of the Constitution in New York:

(a) Benjamin Franklin (b) James Madison (c) Alexander Hamilton (d) George Washington

_____ 18. He authored the large-state plan:

(a) James Madison (b) Alexander Hamilton (c) William Paterson (d) Governeur Morris

_____ 19. He was responsible for the wording of the Constitution:

(a) Robert Morris (b) Benjamin Franklin (c) Governeur Morris (d) George Mason

_____ 20. He developed a system of checks and balances to keep the powers of the three branches of government separate:

(a) Alexander Hamilton (b) George Washington (c) Benjamin Franklin (d) James Madison

CONSTITUTIONAL DELEGATE QUIZ

__b__   1.   He represented Pennsylvania at the Constitutional Convention:
(a) Alexander Hamilton (b) Benjamin Franklin (c) James Madison (d) Oliver Ellsworth

__d__   2.   James Madison was a delegate from:
(a) New York (b) Massachusetts (c) Connecticut (d) Virginia

__a__   3.   New York sent this man to the Constitutional Convention:
(a) Alexander Hamilton (b) James Madison (c) Elbridge Gerry (d) James Wilson

__c__   4.   George Washington was from this state:
(a) New York (b) Massachusetts (c) Virginia (d) New Jersey

__a__   5.   William Paterson represented this state:
(a) New Jersey (b) Pennsylvania (c) Massachusetts (d) Virginia

__b__   6.   He presided over the Constitutional Convention:
(a) Benjamin Franklin (b) George Washington (c) James Madison (d) Alexander Hamilton

__b__   7.   He presented James Madison's Virginia Plan to the Constitutional Convention:
(a) Thomas Jefferson (b) Edmund Randolf (c) George Washington (d) William Patterson

__d__   8.   The small-state plan was supported by:
(a) James Madison (b) Benjamin Franklin (c) Alexander Hamilton (d) William Patterson

__c__   9.   George Mason is known for his advocacy of:
(a) the large-state plan (b) the small-state plan (c) a Bill of Rights (d) a return to the Articles of Confederation

__b__   10. He is called the "Father of the Constitution":
(a) George Washington (b) James Madison (c) Benjamin Franklin (d) Alexander Hamilton

__c__   11. He was the law teacher of John Marshall, James Madison, and Thomas Jefferson:
(a) James Wilson (b) Roger Sherman (c) George Wyth (d) Edmund Randolf

__a__   12. He was a big businessman who wanted a strong central government with the power to tax:
(a) Robert Morris (b) George Mason (c) William Paterson (d) William Samuel Johnson

__c__   13. He is credited with coming up with the Great Compromise, a two-house legislature:
(a) William Paterson (b) James Madison (c) Roger Sherman (d) Alexander Hamilton

__d__   14. He held a Doctor of Laws degree from Oxford University:
(a) Alexander Hamilton (b) Benjamin Franklin (c) James Madison (d) William Samuel Johnson

__b__   15. As a merchant, he wanted commerce regulated by a strong central government:
(a) Oliver Ellsworth (b) Elbridge Gerry (c) James Madison (d) Benjamin Franklin

__b__   16. His good humor cooled off many an angry delegate:
(a) George Washington (b) Benjamin Franklin (c) Alexander Hamilton (d) Oliver Ellsworth

c   17. He advocated a strong, authoritarian central government and fought hard for the ratification of the Constitution in New York:

(a) Benjamin Franklin (b) James Madison (c) Alexander Hamilton (d) George Washington

a   18. He authored the large-state plan:

(a) James Madison (b) Alexander Hamilton (c) William Paterson (d) Governeur Morris

c   19. He was responsible for the wording of the Constitution:

(a) Robert Morris (b) Benjamin Franklin (c) Governeur Morris (d) George Mason

d   20. He developed a system of checks and balances to keep the powers of the three branches of government separate:

(a) Alexander Hamilton (b) George Washington (c) Benjamin Franklin (d) James Madison

Title:	REFORMS IN ENGLISH HISTORY THAT FORESHADOWED ELEMENTS IN THE CONSTITUTION OF THE UNITED STATES
Subject Area(s):	US history, civics
Skills:	Classifying, analyzing, cause and effect relationships
Completion Time:	30 minutes for class discussion of the reform; home study, 20 minutes for taking a quiz
Objective:	For students to trace the origins of many of the ideas found in the Constitution
Comments:	Students should be encouraged to see relationships between English reform ideas and ideas found in the Constitution. The fact that most of the delegates to the Constitutional Convention were familiar with these English reforms should be mentioned.
Materials:	Reform charts, quiz papers, pen, pencil
References:	English history books, encyclopedias
Extension Activities:	Students could write brief research reports on important reform documents in English history.

REFORMS IN ENGLISH HISTORY THAT FORESHADOWED ELEMENTS IN THE CONSTITUTION OF THE UNITED STATES

King	Reform
Henry II (1154–1189)	* Created grand jury system to investigate and indict wrongdoers and a petit jury to try them * Appointed judges who traveled from one town to another, hearing cases and making decisions * Laid the foundations for the English common law that is the foundation of our law today
John (1199–1216)	* Signed the Magna Carta in 1215 at Runnymeade, which stated that 1. no freeman would be imprisoned or his property taken away until he had been tried by a jury of his equals, 2. justice could not be bought or sold, and 3. taxation could be levied only with the consent of the Great Council (important nobles and church officials). These provisions were later extended to the common people.
Henry III (1216–1272)	* Signed the Provision of Oxford (1258), which handed over the powers of government to a small group of nobles * Later, when Simon de Montfort seized him as a prisoner, he enlarged the Great Council with two knights from each shire and two citizens from each town (1265)
Edward I (1272–1307)	* Adopted de Montfort's form of parliament, which was known as the *Model Parliament* (1295) and included nobles, clergy, townsmen, and representatives of the shires

Charles I (1625–1649)	* Parliament forced Charles to accept the *Petition of Right* (1628) by which he promised 1. not to levy further taxes without the consent of Parliament, 2. not to order arbitrary imprisonment, 3. not to quarter troops in private houses, and 4. not to impose martial law in time of peace
Charles II (1660–1685)	* Signed the *Habeas Corpus Act* (1679), which provided that no person could be held in prison without being brought before a judge within a specific time and told the charges against him
William & Mary (1689–1702)	* Signed the *Bill of Rights* (1689), which provided that 1. the king could not suspend laws, levy taxes, or maintain an army without the consent of Parliament; 2. Parliament should meet often; its members were to be freely elected and allowed freedom in their debates; 3. the people were entitled to petition their ruler without fear of persecution; 4. those charged with crimes were guaranteed a jury trial; and 5. cruel or unusual punishments and excessive bails and fines were outlawed.

QUIZ ON ENGLISH REFORMS

_____   1. The Bill of Rights (1689) was signed by:
(a) Henry II (b) William and Mary (c) Henry II (d) Edward I

_____   2. The prohibition against cruel or unusual punishments came out of the:
(a) Bill of Rights (b) Magna Carta (c) Model Parliament (d) Provision of Oxford

_____   3. Charles II signed the:
(a) Bill of Rights (b) Petition of Right (c) Magna Carta (d) Habeas Corpus Act

_____   4. He signed the Magna Carta in 1215:
(a) Henry III (b) Charles I (c) John (d) Charles II

_____   5. The grand jury system was created under:
(a) John (b) Henry II (c) Charles I (d) Charles II

_____   6. That justice could not be bought or sold is a provision of the:
(a) Magna Carta (b) Petition of Right (c) Provision of Oxford (d) Bill of Rights

_____   7. Parliament forced this king to sign the Petition of Right:
(a) John (b) Charles I (c) Edward I (d) Henry III

_____   8. He appointed judges who traveled from town to town to hear cases:
(a) Charles (b) John (c) Henry II (d) Henry III

_____   9. He enlarged the Great Council, which developed into Parliament:
(a) Henry II (b) John (c) Edward I (d) Simon de Montfort

_____   10. The people were entitled to petition their ruler without persecution under the:
(a) Bill of Rights (b) Provision of Oxford (c) Petition of Right (d) Magna Carta

_____   11. Members of Parliament were given freedom in their debates under the:
(a) Provision of Oxford (b) Petition of Right (c) Habeas Corpus Act (d) Bill of Rights

_____   12. King Henry III gave his power to a small group of nobles in the:
(a) Habeas Corpus Act (b) Petition of Right (c) Provision of Oxford (d) Magna Carta

_____   13. The Model Parliament developed under this monarch:
(a) Edward I (b) Charles I (c) John (d) Henry II

_____   14. That taxation would be levied only with the consent of the Great Council is a
provision of the:
(a) Petition of Right (b) Magna Carta (c) Provision of Oxford (d) Bill of Rights

_____   15. This document was signed at Runnymeade:
(a) Petition of Right (b) Bill of Rights (c) Habeas Corpus Act (d) Magna Carta

_____   16. He laid the foundation of English common law:
(a) Charles I (b) Charles II (c) John (d) Henry II

_____   17. All those charged with crimes would get a jury trial under the:
(a) Bill of Rights (b) Provision of Oxford (c) Magna Carta (d) Petition of Right

_____   18. You had to be told the charges against you under the:
(a) Bill of Rights (b) Habeas Corpus Act (c) Petition of Right (d) Magna Carta

_____   19. That Parliament should meet often is a provision from the:
(a) Provision of Oxford (b) Petition of Right (c) Bill of Rights (d) Habeas Corpus Act

_____   20. Martial law could not be imposed in times of peace under the:
(a) Provision of Oxford (b) Petition of Right (c) Magna Carta (d) Bill of Rights

QUIZ ON ENGLISH REFORMS

__b__   1. The Bill of Rights (1689) was signed by:
(a) Henry II (b) William and Mary (c) Henry II (d) Edward I

__b__   2. The prohibition against cruel or unusual punishments came out of the:
(a) Bill of Rights (b) Magna Carta (c) Model Parliament (d) Provision of Oxford

__d__   3. Charles II signed the:
(a) Bill of Rights (b) Petition of Right (c) Magna Carta (d) Habeas Corpus Act

__a__   4. He signed the Magna Carta in 1215:
(a) Henry III (b) Charles I (c) John (d) Charles II

__a__   5. The grand jury system was created under:
(a) John (b) Henry II (c) Charles I (d) Charles II

__a__   6. That justice could not be bought or sold is a provision of the:
(a) Magna Carta (b) Petition of Right (c) Provision of Oxford (d) Bill of Rights

__b__   7. Parliament forced this king to sign the Petition of Right:
(a) John (b) Charles I (c) Edward I (d) Henry III

__c__   8. He appointed judges who traveled from town to town to hear cases:
(a) Charles (b) John (c) Henry II (d) Henry III

__d__   9. He enlarged the Great Council, which developed into Parliament:
(a) Henry II (b) John (c) Edward I (d) Simon de Montfort

__a__   10. The people were entitled to petition their ruler without persecution under the:
(a) Bill of Rights (b) Provision of Oxford (c) Petition of Right (d) Magna Carta

__d__   11. Members of Parliament were given freedom in their debates under the:
(a) Provision of Oxford (b) Petition of Right (c) Habeas Corpus Act (d) Bill of Rights

__c__   12. King Henry III gave his power to a small group of nobles in the:
(a) Habeas Corpus Act (b) Petition of Right (c) Provision of Oxford (d) Magna Carta

__a__   13. The Model Parliament developed under this monarch:
(a) Edward I (b) Charles I (c) John (d) Henry II

__b__   14. That taxation would be levied only with the consent of the Great Council is a provision of the:
(a) Petition of Right (b) Magna Carta (c) Provision of Oxford (d) Bill of Rights

__d__   15. This document was signed at Runnymeade:
(a) Petition of Right (b) Bill of Rights (c) Habeas Corpus Act (d) Magna Carta

__d__   16. He laid the foundation of English common law:
(a) Charles I (b) Charles II (c) John (d) Henry II

__a__   17. All those charged with crimes would get a jury trial under the:
(a) Bill of Rights (b) Provision of Oxford (c) Magna Carta (d) Petition of Right

__b__   18. You had to be told the charges against you under the:
(a) Bill of Rights (b) Habeas Corpus Act (c) Petition of Right (d) Magna Carta

__c__   19. That Parliament should meet often is a provision from the:
(a) Provision of Oxford (b) Petition of Right (c) Bill of Rights (d) Habeas Corpus Act

__b__   20. Martial law could not be imposed in times of peace under the:
(a) Provision of Oxford (b) Petition of Right (c) Magna Carta (d) Bill of Rights

Title:	FEDERAL OFFICE HOLDERS LISTED IN THE CONSTITUTION
Subject Area(s):	US history, civics
Skills:	Charting, locating information, classifying
Completion Time:	30 minutes of class discussion of the chart for this lesson; home study for a quiz on the chart; 20 minutes for taking the quiz in class
Objective:	For students to be able to analyze the distinguishing characteristics of the federal office holders listed in the Constitution
Comments:	Students should be reminded of the fact that our Constitution uses an economy of words in describing the structure of our government. Very little information involving job description is included in the Constitution
Materials:	Charts, quiz papers, pen, pencil
References:	The Constitution of the United States
Extension Activities:	Students could write brief biographical sketches of the lives of famous senators, representatives, Supreme Court justices, or presidents.

DATA CHART FOR FEDERAL OFFICE HOLDERS LISTED IN THE CONSTITUTION

Office	Minimum age requirement	Citizenship requirement	Other requirements	Length of term	Method of election or appointment
Representative	25 (Art. I, Sec. 2)	7 years a citizen (Art. I, Sec. 2)	Must be an inhabitant of the state in which he or she is chosen	2 years; no limit on number of terms (Art. I, Sec. 2)	People in each state vote every two years for men and women to represent them in the House of Representatives
Senator	30 (Art. I, Sec. 3)	9 years a citizen (Art. I, Sec. 3)	Must live in the state he or she represents (Art. I, Sec. 3)	6 years; no limit on the number of terms (Art. I, Sec. 3)	Today, senators are elected by voters of their states; elections for senators take place every two years, but at each election only one-third of the senators are elected, so there is always a body of experienced senators left in the Senate to do government work

President (vice president)	35 (Art. II, Sec. 1)	Must have been born in the United States (Art. II, Sec. 1)	Must have lived in the country for at least 14 years (Art. II, Sec. 1)	4 years (Art. II, Sec. 1); a president is limited to two full terms in office (25th Amendment)	The president and vice president are not elected by a direct vote of the people: the state legislatures decide the way in which electors will be chosen and the electors then choose the President; each state has the same number of electors as it has senators and representatives, and the electors make up what is called the electoral college (Art. II, Sec. 1)
Supreme Court justice	Not mentioned	Not mentioned	Not mentioned	Life (good behavior)	Supreme Court justices are appointed by the president with the consent of the Senate (Art. II, Sec. 2)
Justice	Not mentioned	Not mentioned	Not mentioned	Life (good behavior)	Appointed by the president with the consent of the senate (Art. II, Sec. 2)

QUIZ ON FEDERAL OFFICIALS LISTED IN THE CONSTITUTION

_____ 1. They must be at least twenty-five years old to run for office:
(a) senators (b) presidents (c) representatives (d) Supreme Court justices

_____ 2. They must meet a citizenship requirement of nine years:
(a) representatives (b) senators (c) presidents (d) Supreme Court justices

_____ 3. These officials must have lived in the country for at least fourteen years:
(a) presidents (b) senators (c) Supreme Court justices (d) representatives

_____ 4. They may serve a life term:
(a) presidents (b) senators (c) representatives (d) Supreme Court justices

_____ 5. They are chosen by the president:
(a) Supreme Court justices (b) senators (c) representatives (d) vice presidents

_____ 6. When the president chooses officials of the government, he must get the consent of:
(a) the House of Representatives (b) the Senate (c) the Congress (d) the Supreme Court

_____ 7. The president is elected:
(a) directly by the people (b) by the Congress (c) by the Supreme Court (d) by the electors of the fifty states

_____ 8. The Constitution states that the presidential term is:
(a) two years (b) six years (c) four years (d) life

_____ 9. They must be at least thirty years old to hold office:
(a) senators (b) representatives (c) presidents (d) Supreme Court justices

_____ 10. They serve a two-year term:
(a) senators (b) representatives (c) presidents (d) Supreme Court justices

_____ 11. The Constitution does not list requirements of office for these federal office holders:
(a) senators (b) presidents (c) Supreme Court justices (d) representatives

_____ 12. They must meet a citizenship requirement of seven years:
(a) senators (b) Supreme Court justices (c) presidents (d) representatives

_____ 13. They must be at least thirty-five years old to hold office:
(a) presidents (b) representatives (c) senators (d) Supreme Court Justices

_____ 14. Article II, Section 1 of the Constitution deals with the qualifications of this official:
(a) a senator (b) a representative (c) a president (d) a Supreme Court justice

_____ 15. They serve a term of six years:
(a) presidents (b) representatives (c) Supreme Court justices (d) senators

_____ 16. The twenty-second amendment to the Constitution limits a president to:
(a) four terms (b) three terms (c) two terms (d) a life term

_____ 17. This official has the longest term of office allowed by the Constitution:
(a) the president (b) a senator (c) a representative (d) a Supreme Court justice

_____ 18. This official has the shortest term in office under the Constitution:
(a) a senator (b) a representative (c) a president (d) a Supreme Court justice

_____ 19. The electoral college is the group that elects a:
(a) representative (b) senator (c) Supreme Court Justice (d) president

_____ 20. At an election, only one-third of this group is elected:
(a) senators (b) representatives (c) Supreme Court justices (d) members of the electoral college

QUIZ ON FEDERAL OFFICIALS LISTED IN THE CONSTITUTION

___c___   1. They must be at least twenty-five years old to run for office:
(a) senators (b) presidents (c) representatives (d) Supreme Court justices

___b___   2. They must meet a citizenship requirement of nine years:
(a) representatives (b) senators (c) presidents (d) Supreme Court justices

___a___   3. These officials must have lived in the country for at least fourteen years:
(a) presidents (b) senators (c) Supreme Court justices (d) representatives

___d___   4. They may serve a life term:
(a) presidents (b) senators (c) representatives (d) Supreme Court justices

___a___   5. They are chosen by the president:
(a) Supreme Court justices (b) senators (c) representatives (d) vice presidents

___b___   6. When the President chooses officials of the government, he must get the consent of:
(a) the House of Representatives (b) the Senate (c) the Congress (d) the Supreme Court

___d___   7. The president is elected:
(a) directly by the people (b) by the Congress (c) by the Supreme Court (d) by the electors of the fifty states

___c___   8. The Constitution states that the presidential term is:
(a) two years (b) six years (c) four years (d) life

___a___   9. They must be at least thirty years old to hold office:
(a) senators (b) representatives (c) presidents (d) Supreme Court justices

___b___   10. They serve a two-year term:
(a) senators (b) representatives (c) presidents (d) Supreme Court justices

___c___   11. The Constitution does not list requirements of office for these federal office holders:
(a) senators (b) presidents (c) Supreme Court justices (d) representatives

___d___   12. They must meet a citizenship requirement of seven years:
(a) senators (b) Supreme Court justices (c) presidents (d) representatives

___a___   13. They must be at least thirty-five years old to hold office:
(a) presidents (b) representatives (c) senators (d) Supreme Court Justices

___c___   14. Article II, Section 1 of the Constitution deals with the qualifications of this official:
(a) a senator (b) a representative (c) a president (d) a Supreme Court justice

___d___   15. They serve a term of six years:
(a) presidents (b) representatives (c) Supreme Court justices (d) senators

___c___   16. The twenty-second amendment to the Constitution limits a president to:
(a) four terms (b) three terms (c) two terms (d) a life term

___d___   17. This official has the longest term of office allowed by the Constitution:
(a) the president (b) a senator (c) a representative (d) a Supreme Court Justice

___b___   18. This official has the shortest term in office under the Constitution:
(a) a senator (b) a representative (c) a president (d) a Supreme Court justice

___d___   19. The electoral college is the group that elects a:
(a) representative (b) senator (c) Supreme Court justice (d) president

__a__ 20. At an election, only one-third of this group is elected:
(a) senators (b) representatives (c) Supreme Court justices (d) members of the electoral college

Title:	THE CONSTITUTION: CONFLICTS AND COMPROMISES
Subject Area(s):	US history, civics
Skills:	Cause and effect, analyzing, synthesizing
Completion Time:	One standard period
Objective:	For students to recognize the need for compromise in the resolution of conflicts
Comments:	Students might be led by the teacher through one example of a compromise in the formulation of the Constitution and then left to finish the other cases independently
Materials:	Student exercise sheets, pen, pencil
References:	Textbooks in US history or civics
Extension Activities:	Students could make reports on famous compromises in US history. Compromises can be found by looking at treaties concerning boundary settlements, examining slavery issues in the westward expansion of the nation, investigating labor-management settlements of strikes. etc.

THE CONSTITUTION: CONFLICTS AND COMPROMISES

Definition: Compromise: A settlement of differences in which each side makes concessions

Directions: The major controversies arising in the Constitutional Convention were settled by compromises. Complete the table below so that it will be clear to you what the conflict was, what interests were involved on each side, what each side wanted, and how the issue was settled by compromise.

Conflict	Interests involved	Demands of each side	Compromise
How states should be represented in Congress			
Regulation of foreign trade			
The status of slavery under the Constitution			
Regulation of the slave trade			
Election of the president			

THE CONSTITUTION: CONFLICTS AND COMPROMISES

Conflict	Interests involved	Demands of each side	Compromise
How states should be represented in Congress	States with large populations v. States with small populations	* Representation of states in Congress should be based on population * Each state should have the same number of representatives in Congress	A two-house legislature: in the Senate, each state gets two votes, while in the House, representation is based on population
Regulation of foreign trade	Northern states that wanted to protect their manufacturers from foreign competition v. Southern states that wanted to protect their exports from being taxed	* The government should regulate foreign trade * The government should not regulate foreign trade	Congress was given the power to levy tariffs on imports but not on exports

The status of slavery under the Constitution	Non–slave-holding states v. Slave-holding states	* Slaves should not count in determining representation of a state in the House, but they should count for purposes of taxation * Slaves should count the same as free people as the basis for a state's representation in the House, but should not be counted for tax purposes	Three-fifths of the slaves in a state could be counted by the states for representation in the House and for tax purposes
Regulation of the slave trade	Non–slave-holding states v. Slave-holding states	* No more slaves should be brought to the United States * The slave trade should not be restricted by the government	Congress could not restrict the slave trade for twenty years, or until the year 1808

Election of the president	Delegates who wanted Congress to be the Supreme branch of the government v. Delegates who wanted the principle of the separation of powers to be the guide and therefore supported a strong, independent chief executive officer	* Congress should elect the president * The president should be elected by the people	An electoral college would select the president and each state would have as many electors as it had representatives in Congress

Title:	THE PERFECT PRESIDENT: AN EXERCISE IN SYNTHESIZING
Subject Area(s):	US history, civics
Skills:	Synthesizing, conceptualizing, analyzing
Completion Time:	One standard period plus homework
Objective:	For students to identify factors and qualities we look for in a national leader.
Comments:	Students should make their own lists of factors that they feel are important in choosing a national leader. Many of these suggested factors might be added to the given list for this lesson.
Materials:	Pen, paper, exercise sheets
References:	Encyclopedias, textbooks on government
Extension Activities:	Debates over significant factors and qualities that make a perfect president could be held in class. Students could rank presidents from history using the list of factors and qualities from the lesson.

THE PERFECT PRESIDENT: AN EXERCISE IN SYNTHESIZING

Directions: Fill in the required information to build a picture of a perfect president from your point of view. You are free to ignore any item you feel is irrelevant to your image of a perfect president. Also, feel free to add any categories that you feel should be included in the given list.

1. Age:
   Reason(s):

2. Sex:
   Reason(s):

3. Height/body build:
   Reason(s):

4. Racial background:
   Reason(s):

5. Ethnic background:
   Reason(s):

6. Marital status:
   Reason(s):

7. Political party:
   Reason(s):

8. Educational background:
   Reason(s):

9. Previous occupation(s):
   Reason(s):

10. Travel experience:
    Reason(s):

11. He or she should come from what part of the nation (area or state):
    Reason(s):

12. Five important character traits:

A.

Reason(s):

B.

Reason(s):

C.

Reason(s):

D.

Reason(s):

E.

Reason(s):

13. Three key life experiences that would be good for a president to have had:

A.

Reason(s):

B.

Reason(s):

C.

Reason(s):

14. Five major skills that would help to make a person a perfect president:

A.

Reason(s):

B.

Reason(s):

C.

Reason(s):

D.

Reason(s):

E.

Reason(s):

Title:	A SIMPLIFIED OUTLINE OF THE CONSTITUTION OF THE UNITED STATES
Subject Area(s):	US history, civics
Skills:	Outlining, analyzing
Completion Time:	One standard period plus homework
Objective:	For students to comprehend the scope and sequence of elements making up the Constitution
Comments:	Students could be given some basic instruction in outlining procedures and then be given a start on the assignment to make sure that they fully understand their task.
Materials:	Paper for the outline, pen, pencil
References:	The Constitution of the United States
Extension Activities:	For extra credit, students could make a simplified outline of the Articles of Confederation.

Student Handout—Lesson 16

Directions: Make a simplified outline of the Constitution of the United States.

A SIMPLIFIED OUTLINE OF THE CONSTITUTION OF THE UNITED STATES

Preamble (statement of purpose)

Article I: Legislative Department

A.	Section	1	-	Congress
B.	Section	2	-	House of Representatives
C.	Section	3	-	Senate
D.	Section	4	-	Elections & Meeting
E.	Section	5	-	Rules of Procedure
F.	Section	6	-	Privileges and Restrictions
G.	Section	7	-	Method of Passing Laws
H.	Section	8	-	Powers Delegated to Congress

- Section 9   -   Powers Denied to the Federal Government
- Section 10   -   Powers Denied to the States

Article II: Executive Department

A.	Section	1	-	President and Vice-President
B.	Section	2	-	Powers of the President
C.	Section	3	-	Duties of the President
D.	Section	4	-	Impeachment

Article III: Judicial Department

A.	Section	1	-	Federal Courts
B.	Section	2	-	Jurisdiction of Federal Courts
C.	Section	3	-	Treason

Article IV: Relations Among the States

A.	Section	1	-	Official Acts
B.	Section	2	-	Privileges of Citizens
C.	Section	3	-	New States and Territories
D.	Section	4	-	Guarantees to the States

Article V: Methods of Amendment

Article VI: General Provisions

Article VII: Ratification

Amendments

Amendment	1	-	Freedom of Religion, Speech, Press, Assembly, and Petition
Amendment	2	-	Right to Keep Arms
Amendment	3	-	Quartering of Troops

Amendment	4	-	Search and Seizure; Warrants
Amendment	5	-	Rights of Accused Persons
Amendment	6	-	Right to Speedy Trial
Amendment	7	-	Jury Trial in Civil Cases
Amendment	8	-	Bails, Fines, Punishments
Amendment	9	-	Powers Reserved to the People
Amendment	10	-	Powers Reserved to the States
Amendment	11	-	Suits Against States
Amendment	12	-	Election of President and Vice President
Amendment	13	-	Slavery Abolished
Amendment	14	-	Rights of Citizens
Amendment	15	-	Right of Suffrage
Amendment	16	-	Income Tax
Amendment	17	-	Election of Senators
Amendment	18	-	National Prohibition
Amendment	19	-	Women's Suffrage
Amendment	20	-	"Lame Duck" Amendment
Amendment	21	-	Repeal of Prohibition
Amendment	22	-	Two-Term Limit for Presidents
Amendment	23	-	Presidential Electors for District of Columbia
Amendment	24	-	Poll Tax Banned in National Elections
Amendment	25	-	Presidential Disability and Succession
Amendment	26	-	Voting Age Lowered to 18
Amendment	27	-	Congressional Pay

Title:	A FAREWELL ADDRESS FROM AN OUTGOING PRESIDENT
Subject Area(s):	US history, civics
Skills:	Synthesizing, conceptualizing
Completion Time:	90 minutes
Objective:	For students to identify political, social, and economic problems and consider the impacts they may have on the nation
Comments:	Students should have a class discussion and brainstorming session in order to create a list of problems from which to choose the ones that they will use in their speeches
Materials:	Pen, paper, speech outline on board or in the form of a printed handout
References:	News magazines, newspapers, videos, etc.
Extension Activities:	Students could read several presidential farewell addresses in books of famous American speeches.

A FAREWELL ADDRESS FROM AN OUTGOING PRESIDENT

Background Information: A farewell address is not required by the Constitution, but such presidential addresses are often of historical importance. Outgoing presidents have often used these addresses to warn the American people of possible problems and dangers facing them.

In 1791, George Washington used his farewell speech to warn Americans against "permanent alliances" with foreign powers, a large public debt, and the devices of a "small, artful, enterprising minority to control or change the government."

In 1961, President Dwight D. Eisenhower warned the nation about the potentially extraordinary influence of the military-industrial complex on American life.

Directions: Your assignment is to imagine that you are the president of the United States and that you are engaged in the preparation of your farewell address. You may use this outline to prepare your speech:

I.   *Title*: My Farewell Address

II.   *Introduction*: A general uplifting statement that best illustrates the strong points in your record as president. Without going into much detail, tell the listener or reader what you'll be talking about.

III.   *Body*

    A.   A paragraph about what you consider to be your greatest accomplishment while you were in office.

    B.   A paragraph about what you consider to be your second-greatest accomplishment.

    C.   A paragraph warning the nation about present or future problems that will need the attention of America's future leadership.

IV.   *Conclusion*: In the fifth and last paragraph of your speech, leave the listener or reader with a main thought to carry in his or her mind. Your concluding thoughts may be the only ones remembered.

A Suggested List of Possible Present or Future Problems

Political Problems: the rise of new and challenging world powers, campaign finance issues, poor habits of citizens, the national debt, the influence of special interest groups, a stressed educational system, health care, care for senior citizens.

Social Problems: treatment of minorities, social class differences, drug problems, homelessness, crime, childcare, an aging population.

Economic Problems: inflation management, balance of trade, energy problems, affordable housing for low-income families, poor infrastructure.

Title:	CHART OF THE STRUCTURE OF THE NATIONAL GOVERNMENT UNDER THE CONSTITUTION
Subject Area(s):	US history, civics
Skills:	Synthesis, examination of a document
Completion Time:	About 20 minutes
Objective:	For students to visualize the basic structure of America's national government
Comments:	Students would see how the principle of the separation of powers was put into practice
Materials:	Student sheet, pen, pencil
References:	The Constitution of the United States
Extension Activities:	Students could chart their state government and compare it to the chart for the national government.

CHART OF THE STRUCTURE OF THE NATIONAL GOVERNMENT UNDER THE CONSTITUTION

Directions: Using the letter codes for each item in the given list of terms, fill in the appropriate circles of this structure of national government chart.

Term	Code
THE EXECUTIVE DEPARTMENT	ED
THE JUDICIAL DEPARTMENT	JD
THE VICE-PRESIDENT	VP
THE HOUSE OF REPRESENTATIVES	H
THE SUPREME COURT	SC
SUPREME COURT JUSTICE	J
THE LEGISLATIVE DEPARTMENT	LD
THE PRESIDENT	P
THE CONGRESS	C
THE SENATE	S
THE CHIEF JUSTICE	CHJ
THE US GOVERNMENT	USG

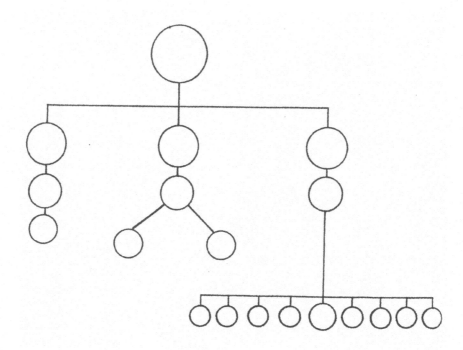

Answer Sheet — Lesson 18

Chart of the Structure of the National Government under the Constitution

Directions: Using the letter codes for each item in the given list of terms, fill in the appropriate circles of this structure of national government chart.

Term	Code
THE EXECUTIVE DEPARTMENT	ED
THE JUDICIAL DEPARTMENT	JD
THE VICE-PRESIDENT	VP
THE HOUSE OF REPRESENTATIVES	H
THE SUPREME COURT	SC
SUPREME COURT JUSTICE	J
THE LEGISLATIVE DEPARTMENT	LD
THE PRESIDENT	P
THE CONGRESS	C
THE SENATE	S
THE CHIEF JUSTICE	CHJ
THE US GOVERNMENT	USG

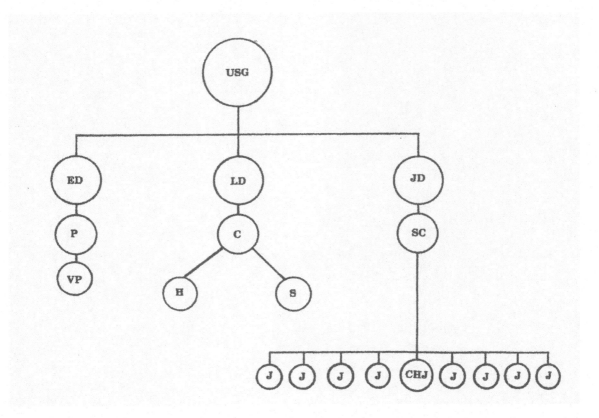

99

Title:	CONSTITUTIONAL POWER GRID
Subject Area(s):	US history, Civics
Skills:	Locating information, analyzing
Completion Time:	One standard period
Objective:	For students to comprehend power relationships found in the Constitution
Comments:	The teacher might do the first exercise to get the class started
Materials:	Copies of the Constitution Power Grid exercise sheet, pen, pencil
References:	The Constitution of the United States
Extension Activities:	Students could provide the Constitutional references by article and section number that support their answers

CONSTITUTIONAL POWER GRID

Directions: For each power listed (1–20), place an (x) in the column that shows the power holder

POWER HOLDERS

POWERS	PRESIDENT	VICE-PRESIDENT	CONGRESS	HOUSE	SENATE	CHIEF JUSTICE
1 NEW STATES MAY BE ADMITTED						
2 GRANTS REPRIEVES AND PARDONS						
3 HAS SOLE POWER OF IMPEACHMENT						
4 CAN LEVY AND COLLECT TAXES						
5 MUST APPROVE A SUPREME COURT JUSTICE						
6 CAN SUCCEED THE PRESIDENT						
7 PRESIDENT OF THE SENATE						
8 NOMINATES AMBASSADORS						
9 CHOOSES A "SPEAKER"						
10 SOLE POWER TO TRY IMPEACHMENTS						
11 CAN BORROW MONEY						
12 PRESIDES OVER PRESIDENT'S IMPEACHMENT TRIAL						
13 CHOOSES A "PRESIDENT PRO TEMPORE"						
14 ALL REVENUE BILLS START HERE						
15 COMMANDS THE ARMED FORCES						
16 MUST GIVE ADVICE AND CONSENT ON TREATIES						
17 DECLARES WAR						
18 NOMINATES SUPREME COURT JUDGES						
19 BREAKS TIE IN SENATE						
20 HEADS THE SUPREME COURT						

CONSTITUTIONAL POWER GRID

POWER HOLDERS

Directions: For each power listed (1 - 20), place an (x) in the column which shows the power holder

POWERS	PRESIDENT	VICE-PRESIDENT	CONGRESS	HOUSE	SENATE	CHIEF JUSTICE
1. NEW STATES MAY BE ADMITTED			x			
2. GRANTS REPRIEVES AND PARDONS	x					
3. HAS SOLE POWER OF IMPEACHMENT				x		
4. CAN LEVY AND COLLECT TAXES			x			
5. MUST APPROVE A SUPREME COURT JUSTICE					x	
6. CAN SUCCEED THE PRESIDENT		x				
7. PRESIDENT OF THE SENATE		x				
8. NOMINATES AMBASSADORS	x					
9. CHOOSES A "SPEAKER"				x		
10. SOLE POWER TO TRY IMPEACHMENTS					x	
11. CAN BORROW MONEY			x			
12. PRESIDES OVER PRESIDENT'S IMPEACHMENT TRIAL						x
13. CHOOSES A "PRESIDENT PRO TEMPORE"					x	
14. ALL REVENUE BILLS START HERE				x		
15. COMMANDS THE ARMED FORCES	x					
16. MUST GIVE ADVICE AND CONSENT ON TREATIES					x	
17. DECLARES WAR			x			
18. NOMINATES SUPREME COURT JUDGES	x					
19. BREAKS TIE IN SENATE		x				
20. HEADS THE SUPREME COURT						x

Title: DATA LOCATION GRID: AN EXERCISE FOR UNDERSTANDING THE DIVISIONS OF THE CONSTITUTION OF THE UNITED STATES

Subject Area(s): US history, civics

Skills: Locating information, analyzing

Completion Time: One standard period

Objective: For students to be able to broadly identify the divisions of the Constitution

Comments: The teacher might do the first exercise for this lesson to make sure that the students understand their task

Materials: Grid sheets for students, pen, pencil

References: The Constitution of the United States

Extension Activities: Students could list the section of each article as well as the specific amendment for each item in the exercise.

DATA LOCATION GRID: AN EXERCISE FOR UNDERSTANDING THE DIVISIONS OF
THE CONSTITUTION OF THE UNITED STATES

Directions: Place an (x) in the column which shoes where each item is located in the Constitution

DIVISIONS OF THE CONSTITUTION

DATA FROM THE CONSTITUTION	PREAMBLE	ARTICLE I	ARTICLE II	ARTICLE III	ARTICLE IV	ARTICLE V	ARTICLE VI	ARTICLE VII	AMENDMENTS
1. allows for a federal income tax									
2. tells how a bill becomes a law									
3. shows how to amend the constitution									
4. slavery prohibited									
5. lists congressional powers									
6. lists presidential powers									
7. rights and duties of the states are discussed									
8. treason is defined									
9. wish for domestic tranquility is expressed									
10. calls for counting the population (census)									
11. says 9 states must ratify the Constitution									
12. tells how new states may be admitted									
13. The Bill of Rights appears here									
14. lists requirements to be a senator									
15. makes the Constitution the supreme law									
16. limitation of presidential terms									
17. lists presidential duties									
18. lists requirements to be president									
19. establishes a Supreme Court									
20. seeks the blessings of liberty to ourselves . . .									

DATE LOCATION GRID: AN EXERCISE FOR UNDERSTANDING THE DIVISIONS OF THE CONSTITUTION OF THE UNITED STATES

Directions: Place an (x) in the column which shows where each item is located in the Constitution

DIVISIONS OF THE CONSTITUTION

DATA FROM THE CONSTITUTION	PREAMBLE	ARTICLE I	ARTICLE II	ARTICLE III	ARTICLE IV	ARTICLE V	ARTICLE VI	ARTICLE VII	AMENDMENTS
1. allows for a federal income tax									x
2. tells how a bill becomes a law		x							
3. shows how to amend the constitution						x			
4. slavery prohibited									x
5. lists congressional powers		x							
6. lists presidential powers			x						
7. rights and duties of the states are discussed					x				
8. treason is defined				x					
9. wish for domestic tranquility is expressed	x								
10. calls for counting the population (census)		x							
11. says 9 states must ratify the Constitution								x	
12. tells how new states may be admitted					x				
13. The Bill of Rights appears here									x
14. lists requirements to be a senator		x							
15. makes the Constitution the supreme law							x		
16. limitation of presidential terms									x
17. lists presidential duties			x						
18. lists requirements to be president			x						
19. establishes a Supreme Court				x					
20. seeks the blessings of liberty to ourselves . . .	x								

Title:	"WHAT'S WRONG?": FINDING ERRORS IN MISQUOTATIONS FROM THE CONSTITUTION
Subject Area(s):	US history, civics
Skills:	Critical reading, locating information, classifying
Completion Time:	One standard period
Objective:	For students to critically analyze a passage from a written work
Comments:	The teacher might provide the class with an example of how the chart should be filled out to get the students started on their task with little difficulty
Materials:	Chart outlines, pen, pencil
References:	The Constitution of the United States
Extension Activities:	Students could make up their own misquotations and exchange them with classmates for extra practice.

"WHAT'S WRONG?" FINDING ERRORS IN MISQUOTATIONS FROM THE CONSTITUTION

Directions: There is one error in each of the following ten misquotations from the Constitution. The error could be an added word or phrase (addition), a changed word or phrase (modification), or a word or phrase left out (deletion). our task is to complete the chart below for this lesson by first, determining the nature of the error in the quotation; second, writing down what the error was; and third, writing down what place the quotation came from in the Constitution.

"WHAT'S WRONG?" CHART OF QUOTATIONS FROM THE CONSTITUTION

Misquotation	Nature of error (addition, modification, deletion)	Error (word or phrase)	Where quotation is found in the Constitution (Preamble, Article, Section, Amendment)

1.	"The United States shall guarantee to every state in this union, a democratic form of government … "			
2.	"The right of citizens of the United States, who are eighteen years of age or older, to vote shall not be denied or abridged by the United States or any state, county, town or city on account of age."			
3.	"We the People of the United States, in order to form a more perfect Union. promote the General Welfare, and secure the Blessings of Liberty to ourselves and our Posterity, do ordain and establish this Constitution for the United States of America"			
4.	"No person shall be convicted of treason unless on the testimony of three witnesses to the same overt act, or on confession in open court."			
5.	"The House of Representatives shall choose their speaker, President and other officers, and shall have the sole power of impeachment."			
6.	"The President shall be commander in chief of the army of the United States, and of the militia of the several states … "			
7.	"The Congress, whenever three-fourths of both houses shall deem it necessary, shall propose amendments to this constitution … "			
8.	"Congress shall make no law respecting an establishment of religion, or prohibiting the free exercise thereof; or abridging the freedom of speech; or the right of the people peaceably to assemble, and to petition the government for a redress of grievances."			
9.	"All bills for raising revenue or taxing the people shall originate in the House of Representatives;"			
10.	"No person shall be elected to the office of the President more than twice, and no person who has held the office of President, or acted as President, for more than two years of a term to which some other person was elected President more than twice."			

Answer Sheet—Lesson 21

"WHAT'S WRONG?" FINDING ERRORS IN MISQUOTATIONS FROM THE CONSTITUTION

Directions: In each of the following ten misquotations from the Constitution, there is one error. The error could be an added word or phrase (addition, a change word or phrase (modification), or a word or phrase left out (deletion). Your task is to complete the chart below for this lesson by first, determining the nature of the error in the quotation; second, writing down what the error was; and third, writing down what place the quotation came from in the Constitution.

"WHAT'S WRONG?" CHART OF QUOTATIONS FROM THE CONSTITUTION

Misquotation		Nature of error (addition, modification, or deletion)	Error (word or phrase)	Where quotation is found in the Constitution (Preamble, Article, Section, Amendment)
1.	"The United States shall guarantee to every state in this union, a democratic form of government … "	modification	"democratic" should read "republican"	Article IV, Section 4
2.	"The right of citizens of the United States, who are eighteen years of age or older, to vote shall not be denied or abridged by the United States or any state, county, town or city on account of age."	addition	"county, town or city" does not appear in the Constitution"Twenty-sixth Amendment	
3.	"We the People of the United States, in order to form a more perfect Union, Promote the General Welfare, and secure the Blessings of Liberty to ourselves and our Posterity, do ordain and establish this Constitution for the United States of America"	deletion	"establish Justice, insure domestic Tranquility, provide for the common defence" was omitted from the original passage	Preamble
4.	"No person shall be convicted of treason unless on the testimony of three witnesses to the same overt act, or on confession in open court."	modification	"three" should read "two"	Article III, Section 3

109

5.	"The House of Representatives shall choose their speaker, President and other officers, and shall have the sole power of impeachment."	addition	"President" should not appear	Article I, Section 2
6.	"The President shall be commander in chief of the army of the United States, and of the militia of the several states ... "	deletion	"and navy" was omitted in quoting from the Constitution	Article II, Section 2
7.	"The Congress, whenever three-fourths of both houses shall deem it necessary, shall propose amendments to this constitution... "	modification	"three-fourths" should read "two-thirds"	Article V
8.	"Congress shall make no law respecting an establishment of religion, or prohibiting the free exercise thereof; or abridging the freedom of speech; or the right of the people peaceably to assemble, and to petition the government for a redress of grievances"	deletion	"or of the press" was omitted from this passage	First Amendment
9.	"All bills for raising revenue or taxing the people shall originate in the House of Representatives;"	addition	"or taxing the people" should not appear	Article I, Section 7
10.	"No person shall be elected to the office of the President more than twice, and no person who has held the office of President, or acted as President, for more than two years of a term to which some other person was elected President more than twice."	modification	the last word in the passage, "twice," should read "once"Twenty-second Amendment	

Title:	LET'S GET THINGS IN ORDER: AN EXERCISE IN CLASSIFICATION
Subject Area(s):	US history, civics
Skills:	Classification, locating information
Completion Time:	One standard period
Objective:	For students to develop a vocabulary of constitutional terms
Comments:	Students should be reminded that many words and phrases in this lesson provide clues to their location in the Constitution. For example, since the President must be "natural born," a look at Article II might be in order.
Materials:	Chart outlines, pen, pencil
References:	The Constitution of the United States
Extension Activities:	Students could make up a different word and phrase list to help the teacher in constructing a second exercise patterned along the lines of this lesson.

LET'S GET THINGS IN ORDER: AN EXERCISE IN CLASSIFICATION

Directions: Read over the list shown below of words and phrases from the Constitution. Then place each word or phrase under the correct heading in the table below. Use the Constitution as your guide. There is a penalty for guessing: every misplaced word or phrase takes one point off your score.

Word/Phrase List: "a more perfect union" … "involuntary servitude" … "reprieves and pardons" … "Full faith and credit" … "shall choose their speaker" … "propose amendments" … "income tax" … "No religious test" … "establish Justice" … "quorum" … "journal" … "corruption of blood" … "grand jury" … "ratification" … "during good behaviour" … "advice and consent" … "supreme law" … "pro tempore" … "original jurisdiction" … "natural born citizen" … "bear arms" … "the chief justice shall preside" … "executive departments" … "revenue" … "excessive bail"

"LET'S GET THINGS IN ORDER" CHART

Preamble	Article I	Article II	Article III	Article IV	Article V	Article VI	Article VII	Amendments

"LET'S GET THINGS IN ORDER": AN EXERCISE IN CLASSIFICATION

Directions: Read over the list shown below of words and phrases from the Constitution. Then place each word or phrase under the correct heading in the table below. Use the Constitution as your guide. There is a penalty for guessing: every misplaced word or phrase takes one point off your score.

Word/Phrase List: "a more perfect union" … "involuntary servitude" … "reprieves and pardons" … "Full faith and credit" … "shall choose their speaker" … "propose amendments" … "income tax" … "no religious test" … "establish Justice" … "quorum" … "journal" … "corruption of blood" … "grand jury" … "ratification" … "during good behaviour" … "advice and consent" … "supreme law" … "pro tempore" … "Original jurisdiction" … "natural born citizen" … "bear arms" … "the chief justice shall preside" … "executive departments" … "revenue" … "excessive bail"

"LET'S GET THINGS IN ORDER" CHART

Preamble	Article I	Article II	Article III	Article IV	Article V	Article VI	Article VII	Amendments
"a more perfect Union"	"shall choose their speaker"	"advice and consent"	"during good behaviour"	"Full faith and credit"	"propose amendments"	"supreme law"	"ratification"	"income tax"
"establish Justice"	"pro tempore"	"executive departments"	"original jurisdiction"			"no religious test"		"excessive bail"
	"the chief justice shall preside"	"natural born citizen"	"corruption of blood"					"bear arms"
		"reprieves and pardons"						"grand jury"
	"revenue"							"involuntary servitude"
	"journal"							
	"quorum"							

113

Title:	THE ARTICLES OF CONFEDERATION AND THE CONSTITUTION OF THE UNITED STATES: A CAUSE AND EFFECT RELATIONSHIP
Subject Area(s):	US history, civics
Skills:	Locating information, cause-and-effect relationships
Completion Time:	One standard period
Objective:	For students to compare political documents looking for causes and effects
Comments:	The teacher might lead the class through the first entry in the chart for this lesson to make sure that the students understand their task.
Materials:	Chart outlines, pen, pencil
References:	The Constitution of the United States
Extension Activities:	Using an overhead projector, the teacher might show the class a copy of the complete Articles of Confederation.

THE ARTICLES OF CONFEDERATION AND THE CONSTITUTION OF THE UNITED STATES: A CAUSE-AND-EFFECT RELATIONSHIP

CAUSE-AND-EFFECT RELATIONSHIP CHART

Directions: Briefly describe how each weakness in the Articles of Confederation shown in the chart below was remedied in the Constitution. In addition to your description, indicate the article and, when necessary, the section and clause from which you got your information.

WEAKNESSES OF THE ARTICLES OF CONFEDERATION, AS SEEN BY MANY DELEGATES AT THE CONSTITUTIONAL CONVENTION	REMEDY
1. Congress was under the control of the state legislatures. The states paid their delegates and could recall them at any time.	
2. Congress was made up of one house in which each state, regardless of its population, had one vote.	
3. There was no independent executive to carry out the laws passed by Congress.	
4. There was no national court system.	
5. Congress had no power to lay or collect taxes.	

6.	Congress could not regulate trade among the states or with foreign nations.	
7.	Congress needed the approval of nine of the thirteen states, a two-thirds majority, to enter into treaties, borrow or coin money, or decide the size of the armed forces.	
8.	Congress could not force obedience to its resolutions or to the Articles of Confederation.	
9.	The Articles of Confederation could be changed only with the consent of all thirteen states.	
10.	Delegates were elected for a one-year term; reelection was possible for no more than three years in every six.	

THE ARTICLES OF CONFEDERATION AND THE CONSTITUTION OF THE UNITED STATES: A CAUSE-AND-EFFECT RELATIONSHIP

CAUSE-AND-EFFECT RELATIONSHIP CHART

Directions: Briefly describe how each weakness in the Articles of Confederation shown in the chart below was remedied in the Constitution . In addition to your description, indicate the article and, when necessary, the section and clause from which you got your information.

WEAKNESSES OF THE ARTICLES OF CONFEDERATION, AS SEEN BY MANY DELEGATES AT THE CONSTITUTIONAL CONVENTION		REMEDY
1.	Congress was under the control of the state legislatures. The states paid their delegates and could recall them at any time.	Senators and representatives receive compensation paid out of the Treasury of the United States. Article I, Section 6
2.	Congress was made up of one house in which each state, regardless of its population, had one vote.	The Congress of the United States consists of a Senate and a House of Representatives. Article I, Section 1 In the House of Representatives, a state's representation is based on its population. Artic I, Section 2, Clause 3
3.	There was no independent executive to carry out the laws passed by Congress.	Executive power was vested in a president of the United States. Article II, Section 1
4.	There was no national court system.	The judicial power of the United States was vested in one supreme court and in inferior courts that the Congress might create. Article III, Section 1

5.	Congress had no power to lay or collect taxes.	Congress was given the power to lay and collect taxes. Article I, Section 8, Clause 1
6.	Congress could not regulate trade among the states or with foreign nations.	Congress was given the power to regulate commerce with foreign nations and among the several states. Article I, Section 8, Clause 3
7.	Congress needed the approval of nine of the thirteen states, a two-thirds majority, to enter into treaties, borrow or coin money, or decide the size of the armed forces.	A two-thirds vote is necessary to override a president's disapproval of a bill; otherwise, a majority vote in each house is sufficient for passage of a bill. Article I, Section 7, Clause 2
8.	Congress could not force obedience to its resolutions or to the Articles of Confederation.	The President must see to it that the laws are faithfully executed. Article II, Section 3 The Constitution is the supreme law of the land. Article VI
9.	The Articles of Confederation could be changed only with the consent of all thirteen states.	Two-thirds of each house of Congress or a convention in two-thirds of the states can propose amendments to the Constitution, which must be ratified by three-fourths of the state legislatures or by conventions in three-fourths of the states. Article V
10.	Delegates were elected for a one-year term; reelection was possible for no more than three years in every six.	Representatives have a two-year term with no restrictions on reelection. Article I, Section 2, Clause 1 Senators serve a six-year term with no restrictions on reelection. Article I, Section 3, Clause 1

Title:	STUDY OF A TREATY
Subject Area(s):	History (US/world), civics
Skills:	Library research, cause and effect, analyzing
Completion Time:	One standard period plus appropriate homework time
Objective:	For students to recognize cause-and-effect relationships
Comments:	Treaties, or agreements between and among nations, are central to international relations. Students might engage in making a list of treaties made under the Constitution by using their textbooks or the list below in order to select a topic for the brief report required in this lesson.

List of Treaties

Treaty of Washington (1871)
Kellogg-Briand Pact (1928)
Treaty of Wanghia (1844)
Tientsin Treaty (1858)
Burlingame Treaty (1868)
Angell Treaty (1880)
Harris' Treaty (1858)
Jay's Treaty (1794)
Monroe-Pinkney (1806)
Webster-Ashburton (1842)
Oregon Treaty (1846)
Clayton-Bulwer (1850)
Hay-Pauncefote (1900)
Adams-Onis (1819)
Guadelupe Hidalgo (1848)
Kanagawa Treaty (1854)
Security Treaty (1960)
Frelinghuysen-Zavala (J.885)
Bryan-Chamorro (1914)
Hay-Bunau-Varilla Treaty (1903)
North Atlantic Treaty (1949)
Maray-Elgin Treaty (1854)
Rio Pact (1947)

Materials:	Outlines for a study of a treaty, pen, pencil

References: Encyclopedias, textbooks in diplomatic history

Extension Activities: Students could make a chart of major treaties in the history of the United
                     States.

STUDY OF A TREATY

Definition: A treaty is an agreement between or among nations.

The constitutionally approved method of treaty-making by the President: Article II, Section 2, "He shall have the power, by and with the advice and consent of the Senate, to make treaties, provided two-thirds of the senators present concur; ... "

OUTLINE FOR A STUDY OF A TREATY

Directions: Choose a treaty made under the Constitution of the United States and write a brief report on it following the outline below:

1. Name of the treaty

2. The date that the treaty was signed

3. The place where the treaty was signed

4. Participating nations

5. Important persons involved in making of the treaty

6. The problem that the treaty was designed to solve

7. The short-term and/or long-term consequences of the treaty

8. Your source(s) of information

Teacher Instructions—Lesson 25

Title:	SUPREME COURT CASES: A SAMPLING
Subject Area(s):	US history, civics
Skills:	Analyzing, cause and effect
Completion Time:	A block of two standard periods will allow time for study, review and testing
Objective:	For students to recognize the political, economic and social impact of Supreme Court decisions
Comments:	Students should read the cases carefully. The teacher might want to have students make up their own test questions based on the chart for this lesson as a way of stimulating student study and review.
Materials:	Chart handouts, quiz sheets, pen, pencil
References:	Textbooks on government, encyclopedias
Extension Activities:	A good class project might be to have students compile a constitutional case file. Library research time should allow students to find many cases to add to the ones included in this lesson.

A CHART OF SUPREME COURT CASES: A SAMPLING

Case	Year	Brief description	Decision	Historical importance
Marbury v. Madison	1803	William Marbury was appointed by outgoing President Adams to the office of Justice of the Peace. Secretary of State James Madison was supposed to deliver the commission to Marbury but didn't. Marbury asked the Supreme Court to issue a "writ of mandamus," a court order forcing a government official to do something.	Chief Justice John Marshall ruled that the Judiciary Act of 1789 allowing the court to issue writs of mandamus was a threat to the doctrine of the separation of powers among the legislative, executive, and judicial branches of government. He also ruled that Marbury could not be denied his commission.	The right of the Supreme Court to declare a law of Congress unconstitutional and therefore not legal was established.
McCullock v. Maryland	1819	The idea of a national bank was unpopular among many states. Maryland tried to get rid of the bank by demanding that the Baltimore branch pay a $15,000 annual fee. McCullock, a cashier at the branch bank, refused to pay and was sued by the State of Maryland to collect.	Chief Justice Marshall ruled that Congress's power to set up a bank was implied in the Constitution. Maryland was told that it could not tax the bank because that power could be used to destroy the bank.	It was established that in a conflict between state and federal powers, the federal power is supreme.
Dartmouth College v. Woodward	1819	The state of New Hampshire had granted a charter to Dartmouth College, a private school, but then decided to bring the college under public control. The state was granted a new charter and appointed a new set of trustees. The original trustees sued a state representative named Woodward.	The Supreme Court ruled in favor of Dartmouth College. The College's charter was a contract and the state did not have the right to back out of a contract.(see Article I, Section 10)	The legal obligations of contracts were preserved.

Gibbons v. Ogden	1823	The New York legislature gave Robert Fulton and a partner a monopoly on steamboat transportation on the Hudson River. The partners named Aaron Ogden to operate a steamship between New York City and the New Jersey shore. Thomas Gibbons set up a competing line under a license from the federal government. Ogden got an order from a New York state court requiring Gibbons to stop running his boats.	The court said that New York's grant of a monopoly interfered with the power of Congress to regulate interstate commerce.	Congress is unchallenged in its right to regulate commerce between the states. This case helped to expand the legal meaning of commerce. Today, radio and television are regulated under the "commerce clause." (*see* Article I, Section 8, Clause 3)
Dred Scott v. Sandford	1857	In 1846, a black man named Dred Scott and his wife sued for their freedom from slavery in a Missouri court. Scott claimed that he had become a free man in 1834 when his owner brought him to Illinois, a place where slavery was illegal.	The court ruled against Dred Scott. It declared that blacks were not American citizens, and thus had no right to bring suit in federal court. Also, it was illegal to forbid slavery in the western territories. Slaves could be taken anywhere their masters cared to take them.	This decision helped to widen the split between pro- and anti-slavery factions. The Civil War and the subsequent passage of the Thirteenth and Fourteenth Amendments reversed the court's decision.
Plessy v. Ferguson	1896	To challenge the constitutionality of Louisiana law, Homer Plessy, a black man, took a seat in the "whites only" car of a New Orleans train. When asked to move, Plessy refused and was arrested.	The Supreme Court upheld the Louisiana law. The court declared that the Fourteenth Amendment could not have been intended to abolish distinctions based upon color, or to enforce social, as distinguished from political, equality, or a commingling of the two races upon terms unsatisfactory to either. Segregation was permissible by law as long as the separate facilities were equal.	The separate but equal doctrine established by this case held until it was overturned in *Brown v. Board of Education* (1954)

Brown v. Board of Education of Topeka	1954	In 1951, Oliver Brown sued the Topeka Board of Education over a Kansas law that permitted cities to have separate schools for blacks and whites.	The court, led by Chief Justice Earl Warren, unanimously decided in favor of Brown. The court held that racial separation, no matter how equal the facilities, branded minority children as inferior and handicapped their development.	Lent encouragement to the civil rights movement and helped to end segregation in all public places.
Baker v. Carr	1962	In 1959, Charles Baker, a politician from Shelby County, Tennessee, sued Tennessee Secretary of State Joseph Carr. Baker contended that election-district boundaries were unfairly drawn so that farming districts with few people had more advantages than urban districts with large populations.	The court ruled that election districts in any state must be as nearly equal as possible in population so that each vote would have essentially equal weight.	Other states soon reapportioned their legislatures to reflect a shift in power from rural to urban areas.
Roe v. Wade	1973	"Jane Roe" was the name used in court by a divorced Dallas waitress who gave her illegitimate son up for adoption in 1970. She had been denied an abortion by Texas law. Roe's lawyers said that Texas anti-abortion laws were unconstitutional in that they violated Roe's right to privacy.	The right to personal privacy was declared broad enough to encompass a woman's decision as to whether or not to terminate her pregnancy.	The Roe decision overturned restrictive abortion laws in more than forty states.
Johnson v. Transportation Agency	1987	A transportation agency in Santa Clara, California hired a woman with lesser qualifications than a competing man to try to correct imbalances in hiring and promotion. The male worker sued the county on the grounds that the transportation agency's action was discriminatory.	The court said that the transportation agency had the right to hire the female worker over the male to right the imbalance in the work force.	Affirmative action to correct racial, ethnic, and sex imbalances in the work force now stands on stronger legal ground.

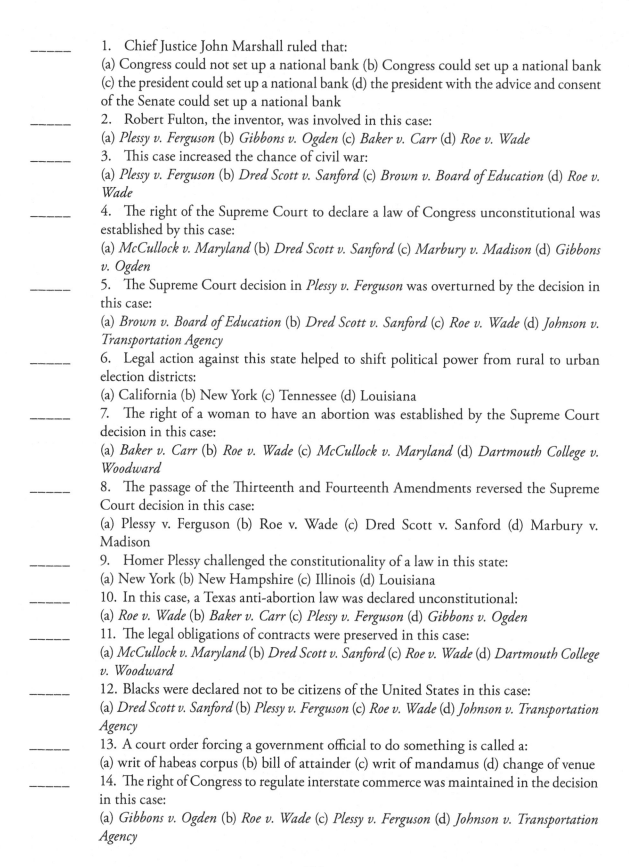

_____ 1. Chief Justice John Marshall ruled that:
(a) Congress could not set up a national bank (b) Congress could set up a national bank (c) the president could set up a national bank (d) the president with the advice and consent of the Senate could set up a national bank

_____ 2. Robert Fulton, the inventor, was involved in this case:
(a) *Plessy v. Ferguson* (b) *Gibbons v. Ogden* (c) *Baker v. Carr* (d) *Roe v. Wade*

_____ 3. This case increased the chance of civil war:
(a) *Plessy v. Ferguson* (b) *Dred Scott v. Sanford* (c) *Brown v. Board of Education* (d) *Roe v. Wade*

_____ 4. The right of the Supreme Court to declare a law of Congress unconstitutional was established by this case:
(a) *McCullock v. Maryland* (b) *Dred Scott v. Sanford* (c) *Marbury v. Madison* (d) *Gibbons v. Ogden*

_____ 5. The Supreme Court decision in *Plessy v. Ferguson* was overturned by the decision in this case:
(a) *Brown v. Board of Education* (b) *Dred Scott v. Sanford* (c) *Roe v. Wade* (d) *Johnson v. Transportation Agency*

_____ 6. Legal action against this state helped to shift political power from rural to urban election districts:
(a) California (b) New York (c) Tennessee (d) Louisiana

_____ 7. The right of a woman to have an abortion was established by the Supreme Court decision in this case:
(a) *Baker v. Carr* (b) *Roe v. Wade* (c) *McCullock v. Maryland* (d) *Dartmouth College v. Woodward*

_____ 8. The passage of the Thirteenth and Fourteenth Amendments reversed the Supreme Court decision in this case:
(a) Plessy v. Ferguson (b) Roe v. Wade (c) Dred Scott v. Sanford (d) Marbury v. Madison

_____ 9. Homer Plessy challenged the constitutionality of a law in this state:
(a) New York (b) New Hampshire (c) Illinois (d) Louisiana

_____ 10. In this case, a Texas anti-abortion law was declared unconstitutional:
(a) *Roe v. Wade* (b) *Baker v. Carr* (c) *Plessy v. Ferguson* (d) *Gibbons v. Ogden*

_____ 11. The legal obligations of contracts were preserved in this case:
(a) *McCullock v. Maryland* (b) *Dred Scott v. Sanford* (c) *Roe v. Wade* (d) *Dartmouth College v. Woodward*

_____ 12. Blacks were declared not to be citizens of the United States in this case:
(a) *Dred Scott v. Sanford* (b) *Plessy v. Ferguson* (c) *Roe v. Wade* (d) *Johnson v. Transportation Agency*

_____ 13. A court order forcing a government official to do something is called a:
(a) writ of habeas corpus (b) bill of attainder (c) writ of mandamus (d) change of venue

_____ 14. The right of Congress to regulate interstate commerce was maintained in the decision in this case:
(a) *Gibbons v. Ogden* (b) *Roe v. Wade* (c) *Plessy v. Ferguson* (d) *Johnson v. Transportation Agency*

_____ 15. Dred Scott sued for:

(a) his right to ride anywhere in a train (b) school desegregation (c) freedom from slavery (d) an end to discrimination in hiring

_____ 16. The decision in this case called for election districts to be as nearly equal in population as possible:

(a) *Roe v. Wade* (b) *Baker v. Carr* (c) *Plessy v. Ferguson* (d) *Gibbons v. Ogden*

_____ 17. This state tried to get rid of the national bank:

(a) Maryland (b) New Hampshire (c) Tennessee (d) Texas

_____ 18. Women's affirmative action rights were upheld by the Supreme Court decision in this case:

(a) *Roe v. Wade* (b) *Baker v. Carr* (c) *Johnson v. Transportation Agency* (d) *Plessy v. Ferguson*

_____ 19. This was **not** a case involving race relations:

(a) *Plessy v. Ferguson* (b) *Dred Scott v. Sanford* (c) *Johnson v. Transportation Agency* (d) *Brown v. Board of Education*

_____ 20. The Supreme Court said that the races could be separated if facilities were equal in this case:

(a) *Dred Scott v. Sanford* (b) *Roe v. Wade* (c) *Gibbons v. Ogden* (d) *Plessy v. Ferguson*

QUIZ SHEET—Lesson 25

  b   1. Chief Justice John Marshall ruled that:
(a) Congress could not set up a national bank (b) Congress could set up a national bank (c) the president could set up a national bank (d) the president with the advice and consent of the Senate could set up a national bank

  b   2. Robert Fulton, the inventor, was involved in this case:
(a) *Plessy v. Ferguson* (b) *Gibbons v. Ogden* (c) *Baker v. Carr* (d) *Roe v. Wade*

  b   3. This case increased the chance of civil war:
(a) *Plessy v. Ferguson* (b) *Dred Scott v. Sanford* (c) *Brown v. Board of Education* (d) *Roe v. Wade*

  c   4. The right of the Supreme Court to declare a law of Congress unconstitutional was established by this case:
(a) *McCullock v. Maryland* (b) *Dred Scott v. Sanford* (c) *Marbury v. Madison* (d) *Gibbons v. Ogden*

  a   5. The Supreme Court decision in Plessy v. Ferguson was overturned by the decision in this case:
(a) *Brown v. Board of Education* (b) *Dred Scott v. Sanford* (c) *Roe v. Wade* (d) *Johnson v. Transportation Agency*

  c   6. Legal action against this state helped to shift political power from rural to urban election districts:
(a) California (b) New York (c) Tennessee (d) Louisiana

  b   7. The right of a woman to have an abortion was established by the Supreme Court decision in this case:
(a) *Baker v. Carr* (b) *Roe v. Wade* (c) *McCullock v. Maryland* (d) *Dartmouth College v. Woodward*

  c   8. The passage of the Thirteenth and Fourteenth Amendments reversed the Supreme Court decision in this case:
(a) *Plessy v. Ferguson* (b) *Roe v. Wade* (c) *Dred Scott v. Sanford* (d) *Marbury v. Madison*

  d   9. Homer Plessy challenged the constitutionality of a law in this state:
(a) New York (b) New Hampshire (c) Illinois (d) Louisiana

  a   10. In this case, a Texas anti-abortion law was declared unconstitutional:
(a) *Roe v. Wade* (b) *Baker v. Carr* (c) *Plessy v. Ferguson* (d) *Gibbons v. Ogden*

  d   11. The legal obligations of contracts were preserved in this case:
(a) *McCullock v. Maryland* (b) *Dred Scott v. Sanford* (c) *Roe v. Wade* (d) *Dartmouth College v. Woodward*

  a   12. Blacks were declared not to be citizens of the United States in this case:
(a) *Dred Scott v. Sanford* (b) *Plessy v. Ferguson* (c) *Roe v. Wade* (d) *Johnson v. Transportation Agency*

  c   13. A court order forcing a government official to do something is called a:
(a) writ of habeas corpus (b) bill of attainder (c) writ of mandamus (d) change of venue

  a   14. The right of Congress to regulate interstate commerce was maintained in the decision in this case:
(a) *Gibbons v. Ogden* (b) *Roe v. Wade* (c) *Plessy v. Ferguson* (d) *Johnson v. Transportation Agency*

__c__ 15. Dred Scott sued for:

(a) his right to ride anywhere in a train (b) school desegregation (c) freedom from slavery (d) an end to discrimination in hiring

__b__ 16. The decision in this case called for election districts to be as nearly equal as possible:

(a) *Roe v. Wade* (b) *Baker v. Carr* (c) *Plessy v. Ferguson* (d) *Gibbons v. Ogden*

__a__ 17. This state tried to get rid of the national bank:

(a) Maryland (b) New Hampshire (c) Tennessee (d) Texas

__c__ 18. Women's affirmative action rights were upheld by the Supreme Court decision in this case:

(a) *Roe v. Wade* (b) *Baker v. Carr* (c) *Johnson v. Transportation Agency* (d) *Plessy v. Ferguson*

__c__ 19. This was **not** a case involving race relations:

(a) *Plessy v. Ferguson* (b) *Dred Scott v. Sanford* (c) *Johnson v. Transportation Agency* (d) *Brown v. Board of Education*

__d__ 20. The Supreme Court said that the races could be separated if facilities were equal in this case:

(a) *Dred Scott v. Sanford* (b) *Roe v. Wade* (c) *Gibbons v. Ogden* (d) *Plessy v. Ferguson*

QUIZ ON THE BILL OF RIGHTS,
AMENDMENTS I THROUGH X

Directions: Identify the following subjects by placing the numbers of the related amendments, I through X, in the spaces provided.

_____ 1. Protects the right to peacefully assemble.

_____ 2. Prohibits being placed in double jeopardy.

_____ 3. Prohibits the infliction of cruel and unusual punishments.

_____ 4. Protects the right to a speedy and public trial.

_____ 5. States that in times of peace, no soldier can be quartered in any home without the consent of the owner.

_____ 6. States that rights not listed or prohibited in the Constitution are reserved to the states.

_____ 7. Guarantees the freedom of speech.

_____ 8. States that an accused person has the right to have legal counsel for his or her defense.

_____ 9. States that a grand jury is necessary to indict a person for a capital or serious crime.

_____ 10. Protects the right to keep and bear arms.

_____ 11. Protects from unreasonable searches and seizures.

_____ 12. Prevents Congress from prohibiting the free exercise of religion.

_____ 13. Guarantees the right to a trail by jury in most suits.

_____ 14. Points out the need for a well-regulated militia.

_____ 15. Prohibits excessive bail and excessive fines.

_____ 16. Guarantees the freedom of the press.

_____ 17. States that in criminal cases, the accused has the right to be confronted with the witnesses against him or her.

_____ 18. States that a person can't be compelled to be a witness against himself or herself.

_____ 19. States that rights not listed in the Constitution are retained by the people.

_____ 20. States that Congress shall make no laws respecting an establishment of religion.

ANSWERS TO THE QUIZ ON THE BILL OF RIGHTS, AMENDMENTS I THROUGH X

Directions: Identify the following subjects by placing the numbers of the related amendments, I through X, in the spaced provided.

I ____   1. Protects the right to peacefully assemble.

V ____   2. Prohibits being placed in double jeopardy.

VIII ____   3. Prohibits the infliction of cruel and unusual punishments.

VI ____   4. Protects the right to a speedy and public trial.

III ____   5. States that in times of peace, no soldier can be quartered in any home without the consent of the owner.

X ____   6. States that rights not listed or prohibited in the Constitution are reserved to the states.

I ____   7. Guarantees the freedom of speech.

VI ____   8. States that an accused person has the right to have legal counsel for his or her defense.

V ____   9. States that a grand jury is necessary to indict a person for a capital or serious crime.

II ____   10. Protects the right to keep and bear arms.

IV ____   11. Protects people from unreasonable searches and seizures.

I ____   12. Prevents Congress from prohibiting the free exercise of religion.

VII ____   13. Guarantees the right to a trail by jury in most suits.

II ____   14. Points out the need for a well-regulated militia.

VIII ____   15. Prohibits excessive bail and excessive fines.

I ____   16. Guarantees the freedom of the press.

VI ____   17. States that in criminal cases, the accused has the right to be confronted with the witnesses against him or her.

V ____   18. States that a person can't be compelled to be a witness against himself or herself.

IX   19. States that rights not listed in the Constitution are retained by the people.

I   20. States that Congress shall make no laws respecting an establishment of religion.

QUIZ ON AMENDMENTS
XI THROUGH XXVII

Directions: Identify the following subjects by placing the numbers of the related amendments, XI through XXVII, in the spaces provided.

_____   1.   Bars immediate pay raises to members of Congress.

_____   2.   Guarantees that citizens' right to vote cannot be denied on account of race, color, or previous condition of servitude.

_____   3.   Prohibits an individual from suing a state in federal court without the state's consent.

_____   4.   Guarantees that a citizen's right to vote cannot be denied "on account of sex."

_____   5.   Lowers the voting age to eighteen.

_____   6.   Requires the Electoral College to vote separately for president and vice president.

_____   7.   Gives Congress the power to collect an income tax.

_____   8.   Prohibits slavery.

_____   9.   Limits a president to two terms.

_____   10.   Declares that no state shall deprive any person of "the equal protection of the laws."

_____   11.   Provides for popular election of senators.

_____   12.   Repeals the Eighteenth Amendment.

_____   13.   Gives citizens of Washington, D.C. the right to vote for president.

_____   14.   Provides for the succession of the president or vice president in the event of death, removal from office, incapacity, or resignation.

_____   15.   Changes the presidential inauguration date from March 4 to January 20.

_____   16.   Prohibits charging citizens a poll tax to vote in presidential or congressional elections.

_____ 17. Gives citizenship to all persons born or naturalized in the United States.

_____ 18. Prohibits the making and selling of intoxicating liquors.

_____ 19. Sets January 3 for the spring date of the assembly of Congress.

_____ 20. Prevents states from depriving any person of "life, liberty, or property, without due process of law."

ANSWERS TO THE QUIZ ON AMENDMENTS
XI THROUGH XXVII

Directions: Identify the following subjects by placing the numbers of the related amendments, XI through XXVII, in the spaces provided.

XXVII   1.   Bars immediate pay raises to members of Congress.

XV   2.   Guarantees that citizens' right to vote cannot be denied on account of race, color, or previous condition of servitude.

XI   3.   Prohibits an individual from suing a state in federal court without the state's consent.

IXX   4.   Guarantees that a citizen's right to vote cannot be denied "on account of sex."

XVI   5.   Lowers the voting age to eighteen.

XII   6.   Requires the Electoral College to vote separately for president and vice president.

XVI   7.   Gives Congress the power to collect an income tax.

XIII   8.   Prohibits slavery.

XXII   9.   Limits a president to two terms.

XIV   10.   Declares that no state shall deprive any person of "the equal protection of the laws."

XVII   11.   Provides for popular election of senators.

XXI   12.   Repeals the Eighteenth Amendment.

XXIII   13.   Gives citizens of Washington, D.C. the right to vote for president.

XV   14.   Provides for the succession of the president or vice president in the event of death, removal from office, incapacity, or resignation.

XX   15.   Changes the presidential inauguration date from March 4 to January 20.

XXIV   16.   Prohibits charging citizens a poll tax to vote in presidential or congressional elections.

XIV __   17.   Gives citizenship to all persons born or naturalized in the United States.

XVIII __   18.   Prohibits the making and selling of intoxicating liquors.

XX __   19.   Sets January 3 for the spring date of the assembly of Congress.

XIV __   20.   Prevents states from depriving any person of "life, liberty, or property, without due process of law."

Student Handout

"QUESTION FILE" ON THE CONSTITUTION OF THE UNITED STATES

Note: Objective true/false, multiple choice, and matching questions make up the body of this "Question File." The questions are derived from the preamble, articles, and amendments that make up the Constitution. The aim is for the teacher to be able to construct a balanced test that cuts across the entire document.

PREAMBLE

TRUE/FALSE:

_____The preamble tells the reason why the people of the United States established the Constitution.

MULTIPLE CHOICE:

_____This was not one of the purposes for establishing the Constitution as stated in the preamble:
(a) to form a more perfect union (b) to establish justice (c) to secure democracy for the people (d) to promote the general welfare
_____The preamble to the Constitution of the United States sets forth the idea that the document will be established by:
(a) delegates (b) the people (c) the Congress (d) the states

MATCHING (match the words that form the correct phrases from the preamble):

_____	1.	insure	a. the common defence
_____	2.	promote	b. justice
_____	3.	secure	c. the blessings of liberty
_____	4.	provide for	d. the general welfare
			e. domestic tranquility

ARTICLE I

TRUE/FALSE:

_____   The Congress represents the executive branch of government.
_____   A representative must be an inhabitant of the state in which he or she is chosen.
_____   A population count of the people (a census) is to be taken every ten years.
_____   No official at an impeachment trial can be convicted without a majority vote of the senators present.
_____   Each state has two senators.
_____   Each house of Congress must keep a journal of its proceedings.

	Nay, or no, votes of the members of either house on any question can be entered in the journal by a one-fifth vote of those present.
_____	During a session of Congress, no house can adjourn for more than three days without the consent of the other.
_____	Senators and representatives are privileged from arrest without exception.
_____	A presidential veto can be overridden by a three-fourths vote of each house.
_____	Patents and copyrights can be issued by Congress to promote the progress of science and useful arts.
_____	The writ of habeas corpus can be suspended if the public safety requires it.
_____	An "ex post facto" law retroactively makes an act a crime.
_____	Titles of nobility can be granted by the United States.

_____ A representative must be at least this old:
(a) twenty years (b) twenty-five years (c) thirty years (d) thirty-five years

_____ Members of the House of Representatives are chosen every:
(a) year (b) second year (c) fourth year (d) sixth year

_____ A representative must have been a citizen of the United States for at least:
(a) four years (b) six years (c) seven years (d) nine years

_____ This body has the sole power of impeachment:
(a) the House of Representatives (b) the Senate (c) the Congress (d) the Supreme Court

_____ The chief officer of the House of Representatives is the:
(a) vice president (b) president pro tempore (c) chief justice (d) speaker

_____ A senator must be at least this old:
(a) twenty years (b) twenty-five years (c) thirty years (d) thirty-five years

_____ A senator must have been a citizen of the United states for at least:
(a) seven years (b) nine years (c) ten years (d) twelve years

_____ A senator has a term of:
(a) two years (b) four years (c) six years (d) eight years

_____ This body has the sole power to try all impeachments:
(a) the House of Representatives (b) the Supreme Court (c) the Congress (d) the Senate

_____ In the Senate, the vice president has:
(a) no vote (b) an unrestricted vote (c) a vote only to break a tie (d) a vote when a majority of the senators present so desire

_____ In the absence of the vice president, the Senate is headed by:
(a) the Speaker (b) the Chief Justice of the Supreme Court (c) the president pro tempore (d) the secretary of state

_____ When the president of the United States is being tried in an impeachment case, this officer must preside:
(a) the vice president (b) the speaker (c) the president pro tempore (d) the Chief Justice of the Supreme Court

_____ There are these many representatives:
(a) 100 (b) 435 (c) 535 (d) 538

_____ Every state gets:
(a) one senator (b) two senators (c) four senators (d) a number of senators based on the state's population

_____ At an impeachment trial, no person can be convicted without the agreement of:
(a) all senators present (b) a majority of the senators present (c) two-thirds of the senators present (d) three-fourths of the senators present

_____ All revenue (money) bills must originate in the:
(a) House of Representatives (b) Senate (c) Supreme Court (d) White House

_____ A presidential veto of a bill passed by Congress can be overridden by a:
(a) two-thirds vote of each house (b) two-thirds vote of the Congress assembled as one body (c) three-fourths vote of each house (d) unanimous vote of each house

_____ Excepting Sunday, the president must return a bill to Congress with his objections within:
(a) two days (b) five days (c) seven days (d) ten days

_____ This is not a power of Congress:

(a) to borrow money (b) to grant pardons (c) to coin money (d) to declare war

_____ The members of Congress number:

(a) 100 (b) 435 (c) 535 (d) 538

_____ Congress can do which one of the following:

(a) pass a bill of attainder (b) pass an ex post facto law (c) suspend the writ of habeas corpus in peace time (d) constitute tribunals inferior to the Supreme Court

_____ Congress can't do which one of the following:

(a) tax articles exported from any state (b) punish counterfeiting (c) establish post offices (d) establish naturalization procedures

_____ No state can do which one of the following:

(a) tax its citizens (b) coin money (c) establish a court system (d) have a constitution

_____ Article I does not discuss which one of the following:

(a) the separation of powers (b) political parties (c) powers forbidden to states (d) how a bill becomes a law

MATCHING:

_____	1. age requirement of twenty-five years	a. senator
_____	2. age requirement of thirty years	b. representative
_____	3. seven-year citizenship requirement	
_____	4. nine-year citizenship requirement	

_____	1. sole power to try impeachment	a. the Senate
_____	2. members chosen every second year	b. the House of Representatives
_____	3. sole power of impeachment	
_____	4. members serve six-year terms	

ARTICLE II

TRUE/FALSE:

_____ The president is commander in chief of the state militias.

_____ The president can grant pardons in impeachment cases (*see* Article II, Section 2)

_____ The president must inform the Congress on the state of the union.

_____ The president can be impeached for and convicted of treason, bribery, or other high crimes or misdemeanors.

MULTIPLE CHOICE:

_____ A presidential term is:
(a) two years (b) four years (c) six years (d) eight years

_____ The term of office for a vice president is:
(a) six years (b) eight years (c) two years (d) four years

_____ The president must be:
(a) seven years a citizen (b) nine years a citizen (c) a natural-born citizen (d) ten years a citizen

_____ The minimum age requirement for a president is:
(a) twenty-five years (b) thirty years (c) thirty-five years (d) forty years

_____ The president can make treaties provided:
(a) a majority of the senators present agree (b) two-thirds of the senators present agree (c) three-fourths of the senators present agree (d) all of the senators present agree

_____ Which one of the following items is not a presidential duty:
(a) delivering a state of the union address (b) commanding the armed forces (c) introducing revenue (money) bills (d) granting reprieves and pardons

_____ The president, vice president, and all civil officers of the United States can be removed from office on impeachment for and conviction of:
(a) treason (b) bribery (c) high crimes and misdemeanors (d) all of these offenses

MATCHING:

_____	1.	pardon	a. agreement
_____	2.	reprieve	b. freedom from a punishment
_____	3.	treaty	c. delay in carrying out a punishment
_____	4.	misdemeanor	d. major crime
			e. minor violation of the law

ARTICLE III

TRUE/FALSE:

_____ Supreme Court justices receive no compensation for their work.

_____ Original jurisdiction means first chance to hear a case.

_____ Impeachment trials are held by a jury.

_____ A person guilty of treason can be punished, but not his family if they are not offenders.

MULTIPLE CHOICE:

_____ Supreme Court justices hold their offices for:
(a) two years (b) four years (c) six years (d) life

_____ No person can be convicted of treason without the testimony of:
(a) one witness (b) two witnesses (c) three witnesses (d) four witnesses

MATCHING:

_____	1.	ratification	a. not part of Article III
_____	2.	how to amend the Constitution	b. part of Article III
_____	3.	treason defined	
_____	4.	the judicial branch of government discussed	

ARTICLE IV

TRUE/FALSE:

_____ A person charged in any state with committing a crime who flees to another state will be returned to the state having jurisdiction over the crime

_____ The citizens of each state are entitled to all privileges and immunities of citizens in all other states.

MULTIPLE CHOICE:

_____ No new states can be formed without:
(a) the consent of the legislatures concerned as well as of the Congress (b) the president's consent (c) Supreme Court approval (d) all of these

_____ The United States guarantees to every state:

(a) a republican form of government (b) a balanced budget (c) social justice (d) the right to tax imports

MATCHING:

_____	1. ratification of the Constitution	a. part of Article IV
_____	2. admission of new states	b. not part of Article IV
_____	3. territorial holdings mentioned	
_____	4. Constitution called supreme law of the land	

ARTICLE V

TRUE/FALSE:

_____ There are two ways of proposing amendments, but only one way of ratifying them.

MULTIPLE CHOICE:

_____ Amendments can be proposed by:
(a) a two-thirds vote of each house of Congress ,or conventions in two-thirds of the states (b) the Supreme Court (c) the president, with the consent of the Senate (d) a popular vote

_____ Amendments are ratified by:
(a) a popular vote (b) three-fourths of the state legislatures, or conventions in three-fourths of the states (c) two-thirds of the state legislatures, or conventions in two-thirds of the states (d) the president, with the consent of the House of Representatives

_____ Article V describes:
(a) the process of ratifying the Constitution (b) the judicial branch of government (c) the amendment process (d) state activities

MATCHING:

_____	1. ratification of the Constitution	a. part of Article V
_____	2. proposing amendments	b. not part of Article V
_____	3. state affairs	
_____	4. ratification of amendments	

ARTICLE VI

TRUE/FALSE:

_____ All officers of the federal government must take an oath to support the Constitution.

MULTIPLE CHOICE:

_____ Article VI says that the Constitution is:

(a) the supreme law of the land (b) the highest law of the nation (c) the country's main body of law (d) the federal law of the United States

MATCHING:

_____ 1. all public officials take an oath to support the Constitution a. part of Article VI
b. not part of Article VI
_____ 2. the legislative branch of government described
_____ 3. the executive branch of government described
_____ 4. the Constitution is established as the supreme law of the land

ARTICLE VII

TRUE/FALSE:

_____ Article VII tells how the Constitution will be ratified.

MULTIPLE CHOICE:

_____ Article VII describes:
(a) the amendment process (b) the ratification process for the Constitution (c) the judicial branch of government (d) the executive branch of government
_____ Article VII says that when this many states ratify the Constitution, it will be established:
(a) seven (b) nine (c) ten (d) thirteen

MATCHING:

_____ 1. call for 9 states to   a. part of Article VII
approve the Constitution   b. not part of Article VII
_____ 2. definition of treason
_____ 3. description of how to amend the Constitution
_____ 4. description of the Constitution as the supreme law of the land

AMENDMENTS

TRUE/FALSE:

_____ Congress can make no law respecting the establishment of religion.
_____ The Fifth Amendment frees us from unreasonable searches and seizures.
_____ A grand jury decides if the evidence in a case warrants a trial.
_____ Suffrage means the right to vote.
_____ The Twentieth Amendment eliminated a long delay between the election and the inauguration of a president.
_____ The Twenty-second Amendment sets a fifteen-year limit on a president's period of service as chief executive officer of the United States.

_____ The vice president has a constitutional way of removing a president he or she feels to be unable to discharge the duties of the office.

MULTIPLE CHOICE

_____ The Bill of Rights is the name applied to the:
(a) First Amendment (b) Tenth Amendment (c) Fifth Amendment (d) first ten amendments

_____ The slaves were freed under this amendment:
(a)Thirteenth (b) Fourteenth (c) Fifteenth (d) Sixteenth

_____ This amendment gave citizens of eighteen years of age the right to vote:
(a) Twenty-second (b) Twenty-fourth (c)Twenty-fifth (d) Twenty-sixth

_____ This amendment limits the president to two terms:
(a) Eighteenth (b) Nineteenth (c) Twenty-first (d) Twenty-second

_____ This amendment gave women the right to vote:
(a) Eighteenth (b) Nineteenth (c) Twentieth (d) Twenty-first

_____ This amendment established a federal income tax:
(a) Fourteenth (b) Fifteenth (c) Sixteenth (d) Seventeenth

MATCHING:

_____	1.	freedom of speech	a. Second Amendment
_____	2.	you don't have to be a witness against yourself	b. Eighth Amendment
			c. Ninth Amendment
_____	3.	no cruel punishment	d. First Amendment
_____	4.	right to bear arms	e. FifthAmendment

_____	1.	prohibition of intoxicating liquors	a. First Amendment
			b. Fourth Amendment
_____	2.	repeal of prohibition	c. Eighteenth Amendment
_____	3.	no poll tax in national elections	d. Twenty-fourth Amendment
			e. Twenty-first Amendment
_____	4.	freedom from search	

_____	1.	presidential disability and succession	a. Twenty-third Amendment
			b. Third Amendment
_____	2.	right to a speedy trial	c. Sixth Amendment
_____	3.	quartering of soldiers	d. Fourth Amendment
_____	4.	votes for residents of the District of Columbia	e. Twenty-fifth Amendment

_____	1.	right of petition	a. Seventeenth Amendment
_____	2.	can't be tried twice for the same crime	b. Thirteenth Amendment
_____	3.	popular election of senators	c. Twenty-fifth Amendment
_____	4.	a disabled president can be emoved from office	d. Fifth Amendment
			e. First Amendment

_____	1.	people have a right to assemble	a. Seventh Amendment
			b. Eleventh Amendment
_____	2.	no excessive bail can be required	c. Twenty-fourth Amendment
			d. First Amendment
_____	3.	states can only be sued in their own courts	e. Eighth Amendment
_____	4.	people have a right to a jury trial	

_____	1.	Twenty-second Amendment	a. deals with voting rights
_____	2.	Nineteenth Amendment	b. deals with curbing powers of the president
_____	3.	Twenty-sixth Amendment	
_____	4.	Twenty-fifth Amendment	

Student Handout

"QUESTION FILE" ON THE CONSTITUTION OF THE UNITED STATES

Note: Objective true/false, multiple choice, and matching questions make up the body of this "Question File." The questions are derived from the preamble, articles, and amendments that make up the Constitution. The aim is for the teacher to be able to construct a balanced test that cuts across the entire document.

PREAMBLE

TRUE/FALSE:

___T___ The preamble tells the reason why the people of the United States established the Constitution.

MULTIPLE CHOICE:

___c___ This was not one of the purposes for establishing the Constitution as stated in the preamble:
(a) to form a more perfect union (b) to establish justice (c) to secure democracy for the people (d) to promote the general welfare

___b___ The preamble to the Constitution of the United States sets forth the idea that the document will be established by:
(a) delegates (b) the people (c) the Congress (d) the states

MATCHING (match the words that form the correct phrases from the preamble):

_e_	1. insure	a. the common defence
_d_	2. promote	b. justice
_c_	3. secure	c. the blessings of liberty
_a_	4. provide for	d. the general welfare
		e. domestic tranquility

ARTICLE I

TRUE/FALSE:

_F_ The Congress represents the executive branch of government.
_T_ A representative must be an inhabitant of the state in which he or she is chosen.
_T_ A population count of the people (a census) is taken every ten years.
_F_ No official at an impeachment trial can be convicted without a majority vote of the senators present.
_T_ Each state has two senators.
_T_ Each house of Congress must keep a journal of its proceedings.

__T__	Nay, or no, votes of the members of either house on any question can be entered in the journal by a one-fifth vote of those present.
__T__	During a session of Congress, no house can adjourn for more than three days without the consent of the other.
__F__	Senators and representatives are privileged from arrest without exception.
__F__	A presidential veto can be overridden by a three-fourths vote of each house.
__T__	Patents and copyrights can be issued by Congress to promote the progress of science and useful arts.
__T__	The writ of habeas corpus can be suspended if the public safety requires it.
__T__	An "ex post facto" law retroactively makes an act a crime.
__F__	Titles of nobility can be granted by the United States.

MULTIPLE CHOICE:

__b__	A representative must be at least this old: (a) twenty years (b) twenty-five years (c) thirty years (d) thirty-five years
__b__	Members of the House of Representatives are chosen every: (a) year (b) second year (c) fourth year (d) sixth year
__c__	A representative must have been a citizen of the United States for at least: (a) four years (b) six years (c) seven years (d) nine years
__a__	This body has the sole power of impeachment: (a) the House of Representatives (b) the Senate (c) the Congress (d) the Supreme Court
__d__	The chief officer of the House of Representatives is the: (a) vice president (b) president pro tempore (c) chief justice (d) speaker
__c__	A senator must be at least this old: (a) twenty years (b) twenty-five years (c) thirty years (d) thirty-five years
__b__	A senator must have been a citizen of the United states for at least: (a) seven years (b) nine years (c) ten years (d) twelve years
__c__	A senator has a term of: (a) two years (b) four years (c) six years (d) eight years
__d__	This body has the sole power to try all impeachments: (a) the House of Representatives (b) the Supreme Court (c) the Congress (d) the Senate
__c__	In the Senate, the vice president has: (a) no vote (b) an unrestricted vote (c) a vote only to break a tie (d) a vote when a majority of the senators present so desire
__c__	In the absence of the vice president the Senate is headed by: (a) the Speaker (b) the Chief Justice of the Supreme Court (c) the president pro tempore (d) the secretary of state
__d__	When the president of the United States is being tried in an impeachment case, this officer must preside: (a) the vice president (b) the speaker (c) the president pro tempore (d) the chief justice of the Supreme Court
__b__	There are these many representatives: (a) 100 (b) 435 (c) 535 (d) 538
__b__	Every state gets: (a) one senator (b) two senators (c) four senators (d) a number of senators based on the state's population

__c__	At an impeachment trial, no person can be convicted without the agreement of: (a) all senators present (b) a majority of the senators present (c) two-thirds of the senators present (d) three-fourths of the senators present
__a__	All revenue (money) bills must originate in the: (a) House of Representatives (b) Senate (c) Supreme Court (d) White House
__a__	A presidential veto of a bill passed by Congress can be overridden by a: (a) two-thirds vote of each house (b) two-thirds vote of the Congress assembled as one body (c) three-fourths vote of each house (d) unanimous vote of each house
__d__	Excepting Sunday, the president must return a bill to Congress with his objections within: (a) two days (b) five days (c) seven days (d) ten days
__b__	This is not a power of Congress: (a) to borrow money (b) to grant pardons (c) to coin money (d) to declare war
__c__	The members of Congress number: (a) 100 (b) 435 (c) 535 (d) 538
__d__	Congress can do which one of the following: (a) pass a bill of attainder (b) pass an ex post facto law (c) suspend the writ of habeas corpus in peace time (d) constitute tribunals inferior to the Supreme Court
__a__	Congress can't do which one of the following: (a) tax articles exported from any state (b) punish counterfeiting (c) establish post offices (d) establish naturalization procedures
__b__	No state can do which one of the following: (a) tax its citizens (b) coin money (c) establish a court system (d) have a constitution
__b__	Article I does not discuss which one of the following: (a) the separation of powers (b) political parties (c) powers forbidden to states (d) how a bill becomes a law

MATCHING:

__b__	1.	age requirement of twenty-five years	a. senator
__a__	2.	age requirement of thirty years	b. representative
__b__	3.	seven-year citizenship requirement	
__a__	4.	nine-year citizenship requirement	

__a__	1.	sole power to try impeachment	a. the Senate
__b__	2.	members chosen every second year	b. the House of Representatives
__b__	3.	sole power of impeachment	
__a__	4.	members serve six-year terms	

ARTICLE II

TRUE/FALSE:

__T__	The president is commander in chief of the state militias.
__F__	The president can grant pardons in impeachment cases (*see* Article II, Section 2).
__T__	The president must inform the Congress on the state of the union.

<u> T </u>   The president can be impeached for and convicted of treason, bribery, or other high crimes or misdemeanors.

MULTIPLE CHOICE:

<u> b </u>   A presidential term is:
(a) two years (b) four years (c) six years (d) eight years

<u> d </u>   The term of office for a vice president is:
(a) six years (b) eight years (c) two years (d) four years

<u> c </u>   The president must be:
(a) seven years a citizen (b) nine years a citizen (c) a natural-born citizen (d) ten years a citizen

<u> c </u>   The minimum age requirement for a president is:
(a) thirty-five years (b) thirty years (c) thirty-five years (d) forty years

<u> b </u>   The president can make treaties provided:
(a) a majority of the senators present agree (b) two-thirds of the senators present agree (c) three-fourths of the senators present agree (d) all of the senators present agree

<u> c </u>   Which one of the following items is not a presidential duty:
(a) delivering a state of the union address (b) commanding the armed forces (c) introducing revenue (money) bills (d) granting reprieves and pardons

<u> d </u>   The president, vice president, and all civil officers of the United States can be removed from office on impeachment for and conviction of:
(a) treason (b) bribery (c) high crimes and misdemeanors (d) all of these offenses

MATCHING:

<u> b </u>	1.	pardon	a. agreement
<u> c </u>	2.	reprieve	b. freedom from a punishment
<u> a </u>	3.	treaty	c. delay in carrying out a punishment
<u> e </u>	4.	misdemeanor	d. major crime
			e. minor violation of the law

TRUE/FALSE:

<u> F </u>   Supreme Court justices receive no compensation for their work.
<u> T </u>   Original jurisdiction means first chance to hear a case.
<u> F </u>   Impeachment trials are held by a jury.
<u> T </u>   A person guilty of treason can be punished, but not his family if they are not offenders.

MULTIPLE CHOICE:

<u> d </u>   Supreme Court justices hold their offices for:
(a) two years (b) four years (c) six years (d) life

<u> b </u>   No person can be convicted of treason without the testimony of:
(a) one witness (b) two witnesses (c) three witnesses (d) four witnesses

MATCHING:

<u> a </u>   1. ratification   a. not part of Article III

<u> a </u>   2. how to amend the Constitution   b. part of Article III

<u> b </u>   3. treason defined

<u> b </u>   4. the judicial branch of government discussed

ARTICLE IV

TRUE/FALSE

<u> T </u>   A person charged in any state with committing a crime who flees to another state will be returned to the state having jurisdiction over the crime.

<u> T </u>   The citizens of each state are entitled to all privileges and immunities of citizens in all other states.

MULTIPLE CHOICE:

<u> a </u>   No new states can be formed without:
(a) the consent of the legislatures concerned as well as of the Congress (b) the president's consent (c) Supreme Court approval (d) all of these

<u> a </u>   The United States guarantees to every state:
(a) a republican form of government (b) a balanced budget (c) social justice (d) the right to tax imports

MATCHING:

<u> b </u>   1. ratification of the Constitution a. part of Article IV

<u> a </u>   2. admission of new states b. not part of Article IV

<u> a </u>   3. territorial holdings mentioned

<u> b </u>   4. Constitution called supreme law of the land

ARTICLE V

TRUE/FALSE:

<u> F </u>   There are two ways of proposing amendments but only one way of ratifying them.

MULTIPLE CHOICE:

<u> a </u>   Amendments can be proposed by:
(a) a two-thirds vote of each house of Congress, or conventions in two-thirds of the states (b) the Supreme Court (c) the president, with the consent of the Senate (d) a popular vote

<u> b </u>   Amendments are ratified by:
(a) a popular vote (b) three-fourths of the state legislatures, or conventions in three-fourths

of the states (c) two-thirds of the state legislatures, or conventions in two-thirds of the states (d) the president, with the consent of the House of Representatives

__c__   Article V describes:
(a) the process of ratifying the Constitution (b) the judicial branch of government (c) the amendment process (d) state activities

MATCHING:

__b__	1. ratification of the Constitution	a. part of Article V
__a__	2. proposing amendments	b. not part of Article V
__b__	3. state affairs	
__a__	4. ratification of amendments	

ARTICLE VI

TRUE/FALSE:

__T__   All officers of the federal government must take an oath to support the Constitution.

MULTIPLE CHOICE:

__a__   Article VI says that the Constitution is:
(a) the supreme law of the land (b) the highest law of the nation (c) the country's main body of law (d) the federal law of the United States

MATCHING:

__a__	1. all public officials take an oath to support the Constitution	a. part of Article VI
		b. not part of Article VI
__b__	2. the legislative branch of government is described	
__b__	3. the executive branch of government is described	
__a__	4. the Constitution is established as the supreme law of the land	

ARTICLE VII

TRUE/FALSE

__T__   Article VII tells how the Constitution will be ratified.

MULTIPLE CHOICE:

__b__   Article VII describes:
(a) the amendment process (b) the ratification process for the Constitution (c) the judicial branch of government (d) the executive branch of government

__b__   Article VII says that when this many states ratify the Constitution it will be established:
(a) seven (b) nine (c) ten (d) thirteen

MATCHING:

__a__	1.	call for nine states to approve the Constitution	a. part of Article VII
			b. not part of Article VII
__b__	2.	definition of treason	
__b__	3.	description of how to amend the Constitution	
__b__	4.	description of the Constitution as the supreme law of the land	

AMENDMENTS

TRUE/FALSE:

__T__	Congress can make no law respecting the establishment of religion.
__F__	The Fifth Amendment frees us from unreasonable searches and seizures.
__T__	A grand jury decides if the evidence in a case warrants a trial.
__T__	Suffrage means the right to vote.
__T__	The Twentieth Amendment eliminated a long delay between the election and the inauguration of a president.
__F__	The Twenty-second Amendment sets a fifteen-year limit on a president's period of service as chief executive officer of the United States.
__T__	The vice president has a constitutional way of removing a president he or she feels to be unable to discharge the duties of the office.

MULTIPLE CHOICE

__d__ The Bill of Rights is the name applied to the:
(a) First Amendment (b) Tenth Amendment (c) Fifth Amendment (d) first ten amendments

__a__ The slaves were freed under this amendment:
(a) Thirteenth (b) Fourteenth (c) Fifteenth (d) Sixteenth

__d__ This amendment gave citizens of eighteen years of age the right to vote:
(a) Twenty-second (b) Twenty-fourth (c) Twenty-fifth (d) Twenty-sixth

__d__ This amendment limits the president to two terms:
(a) Eighteenth (b) Nineteenth (c) Twenty-first (d) Twenty-second

__b__ This amendment gave women the right to vote:
(a) Eighteenth (b) Nineteenth (c) Twentieth (d) Twenty-first

__c__ This amendment established a federal income tax:
(a) Fourteenth (b) Fifteenth (c) Sixteenth (d) Seventeenth

MATCHING:

__d__	1.	freedom of speech	a. Second Amendment
__e__	2.	you don't have to be a witness against yourself	b. Eighth Amendment
			c. Ninth Amendment
__b__	3.	no cruel punishment	d. First Amendment
__a__	4.	right to bear arms	e. Fifth Amendment

__a__	1. prohibition of intoxicating liquors	a. First Amendment
		b. Fourth Amendment
__c__	2. repeal of prohibition	c. Eighteenth Amendment
__d__	3. no poll tax in national elections	d. Twenty-fourth Amendment
		e. Twenty-first Amendment
__b__	4. freedom from search	

__e__	1. presidential disability and succession	a. Twenty-third Amendment
		b. Third Amendment
__c__	2. right to a speedy trial	c. Sixth Amendment
__b__	3. quartering of soldiers	d. Fourth Amendment
__a__	4. votes for residents of the District of Columbia	e. Twenty-fifth Amendment

__e__	1. right of petition	a. Seventeenth Amendment
__d__	2. can't be tried twice for the	b. Thirteenth Amendment
__a__	3. popular election of senators	c. Twenty-fifth Amendment
__c__	4. a disabled president can be removed from office	d. Fifth Amendment
		e. First Amendment

__d__	1. people have a right to assemble	a. Seventh Amendment
		b. Eleventh Amendment
__e__	2. no excessive bail can be required	c. Twenty-fourth Amendment
		d. First Amendment
__b__	3. states can only be sued in their own courts	e. Eighth Amendment
__a__	4. people have a right to a jury trial	

__b__	1. Twenty-second Amendment	a. deals with voting rights
__a__	2. Nineteenth Amendment	b. deals with curbing powers
__a__	3. Twenty-sixth Amendment	of the president
__b__	4. Twenty-fifth Amendment	

CONSTITUTIONAL TOPIC LOCATER

Admiralty and maritime law: Article III, Section 2

Admission of new states: Article I, Section 3; Article IV, Section 1

Advice and consent: Article II, Section 2

African American voting rights: Amendment 15, Section 1; Amendment 24

Age requirements for office holders:
    President: Article II, Section 1
    Senators: Article I, Section 3
    Representative: Article I, Section 2

Ambassadors: Article III, Section 2; Article II, Section 3

Amendment: Article V

Appointments: Article II, Section 2

Bail, excessive: Amendment 8

Bill: Article I, Section 7

Bill of attainder: Article I, Section 9

Bill of Rights: Amendments 1 through 10

Borrowing money: Article I, Section 8

Census: Article I, Section 2

Chief Justice of the Supreme Court, duty in the trial of a president: Article I, Section 3

Church and state: Article VI, Amendment I

Citizenship: Amendment 14

Civil rights: Bill of Rights, Amendments 13, 14, 15, 17, 19, 23, 24, 26

Coin money: Article I, Section 8

Commander in chief: Article II, Section 2

GLOSSARY OF CONSTITUTIONAL TERMS

Note: The authors of the Constitution used "he" exclusively to describe people of both male and female gender. In modern usage it is preferable to use both "he" and "she" as descriptive pronouns. We have followed this practice in this book.

Abolition To do away with something. In the US, this term is associated with the ending of slavery.

Abridge To reduce or contract: to diminish or curtail.

Adjourn To suspend proceedings to another time or place.

Affirmation An assertion that something is true or factual.

Ambassador A diplomatic official of the highest rank appointed and accredited as a representative in residence by one government to another.

Amendment A revision or change.

Appellate Having the power to hear appeals and to review court decisions.

Apportion To divide and assign according to a plan or proportion.

Appropriation Public funds set aside for a specific purpose.

Arsenals Government establishments for the storing, manufacturing, or repairing of arms, ammunition, and other war material.

Articles of Confederation The first plan for a government for the United States of America. It was written and established by the Second Continental Congress in 1775.

Ascertain To discover through examination or experimentation.

Attainder of Treason The loss of all civil rights on a conviction of treason.

Ballot A list of candidates running for office.

Bankruptcy The condition of being legally impoverished.

Bill A proposed law.

Bill of attainder A legislative act pronouncing a person guilty of a crime.

Bill of credit Paper issued by a state as a substitution for money.

Bill of Rights The first ten amendments to the Constitution of the United States.

Bound Under legal or moral obligation; under contract.

Bounties Rewards, inducements, or payments, especially those given by a government for acts beneficial to the state.

Breach of the Peace A violation or disturbance of the public tranquility and order.

Bribery The offering, giving, or receiving, or soliciting of something of value for the purpose of influencing the action of an official in the discharge of his or her public or legal duties.

Capital crime One in or for which a death penalty may, but not necessarily will, be imposed.

Capitation (tax) A poll tax. A tax or imposition upon the person.

Census (official) The count or enumeration of people of a state, nation, district, or other political subdivision.

Chusing An old spelling of choosing.

Citizen A person owing loyalty to and entitled by birth or naturalization to the protection of a given state.

Civil Pertaining to citizens and their relations with the state.

Commander in chief One who holds supreme or highest command of armed forces.

Commerce The buying and selling of goods, especially on a large scale.

Commission The act of granting certain powers or the authority to carry out a particular task or duty.

Compact An agreement or covenant.

Compensation Something given or received as payment or reparation.

Concurrence Agreement in opinion.

Confederation A group of states united for a common purpose.

Congress The national legislative body of the United States, consisting of the Senate and the House of Representatives. The terms "congressman" and "congresswoman" refer to a member of the US Congress, especially the House of Representatives.

Constituency The body of voters represented by an elected official.

Constitution The system of fundamental laws and principles that prescribes the nature, functions, and limits of a government or other institution.

Construed To place a certain meaning on; interpret.

Consuls Officials appointed by a government to reside in a foreign city, represent their government or commercial interests, and give assistance to its citizens there.

Continental Army The name given to the armed land forces created by the Second Continental Congress, which appointed George Washington of Virginia as the commander in chief.

Continental Convention In May, 1787, fifty-five delegates from all the thirteen states except Rhode Island met at a convention in Philadelphia. They came together to discuss how to improve the Articles of Confederation. The delegates soon decided that improvement was not enough: a whole new Constitution was required.

Convention A formal assembly or meeting of members, representatives, or delegates of a group, such as a political party or fraternal society.

Conviction The act or process of finding or proving guilt.

Corruption of blood In old English law, the consequence of attainder (see Bill of Attainder), being that the attained person could neither inherit lands or other wealth from his or her ancestor, nor retain those he or she already had, nor transmit them by descent to any heir, because his or her blood was considered to be corrupted.

Counterfeit To make a copy of something, usually with the intent to defraud; forge; used especially for money.

Delegate A person chosen to act for others in a meeting or for a government.

Devolved To pass something downward, such as a task or responsibility.

Direct tax A tax, such as an income or property tax, levied directly on a taxpayer.

District of Columbia The seat of the US government. It covers sixty-nine square miles along the Potomac River between Maryland and Virginia. The city of Washington covers the entire district.

Double jeopardy The act of putting a person through a second trial for an offense for which he or she has already been prosecuted.

Duties Taxes charged by a government, especially on imports.

Elastic clause Article I, Section7, of the Constitution, which allows Congress to deal with many matters not specifically mentioned in that document.

Elector A person entitled to vote in an election. In the United States, it specifically refers to a member of the electoral college.

Electoral college A group of electors from all the states and the District of Columbia who assemble to perform the duty of voting for a president.

Emancipation The act by which one who was unfree, or under the power and control of another, is rendered free, or set at liberty and made his or her own master.

Eminent domain The power to take private property for public use by the state, municipalities, and private persons or corporations authorized to exercise functions of public character.

Emoluments The profits arising from office, employment, or labor.

Equity Broad principles of reason and justice. Traditionally, courts of law and courts of equity were separate. Today, most courts combine law and equity cases. Courts of equity have the power to order a wrongdoer to stop a harmful act or to order the performance of an act necessary to avoid harm. Today, a court order prohibiting an act is called an injunction and an order requiring that an act be performed is a mandatory injunction.

Excises Internal taxes levied by a law-making branch of government on the production, sale, or consumption of certain commodities, such as tobacco or liquor, within a country.

Executive The branch of government charged with putting into effect the country's laws and administering its functions; the chief officer of a government.

Ex post facto Formulated, enacted, or operating retroactively. Used especially of laws.

Extradition The legal surrender of an alleged criminal to the jurisdiction of another state, country, or government for trial.

Federal A form of government in which a union of states recognizes a central authority while retaining certain powers of government; of or pertaining to the central government of a federation, as distinct from the governments of its member units.

Felonies Any of several crimes, such as murder, rape, or burglary, considered more serious than a misdemeanor and punishable by a more stringent sentence.

Filibuster The use of obstructionist tactics, especially prolonged speechmaking, for the purpose of delaying legislative action.

First Continental Congress Colonial leaders from each colony, except Georgia, met in Philadelphia to decide what to do about the unpopular laws passed by the British. These leaders formed a group called the Continental Congress.

Forfeiture The act of surrendering something as punishment for a crime, offense, error, or breach of contract.

Grand jury A jury of twelve to twenty-three people convened in private session to evaluate accusations against persons charged with crimes and to determine whether the evidence warrants a bill of indictment.

Hereditaments Inherited wealth.

Impeach To make an accusation against.

Imposts Something imposed or levied, as a tax or duty.

Indictment A written statement charging a person with a crime or other offense, drawn up by a prosecuting attorney and approved for trial by a grand jury.

Inferior courts Courts lower in order, degree, or rank than the Supreme Court.

Infringed To violate or go beyond the limits of, for example, a law.

Inhabitant A permanent resident.

Insurrections Acts or instances of open revolt against a government or ruling authority.

Intoxication The inducement, especially by the effect of ingested alcohol, of any of a series of progressively deteriorating states ranging from exhilaration to stupefaction.

Involuntary servitude Services not performed willingly or deliberately.

Judicial Of, pertaining to, or relating to courts of law or to the administration of justice. For example, the judicial branch of government in the United States is the Supreme Court.

Jurisdiction The right and power to interpret and apply the law; the territorial range of authority or control.

Legislative The lawmaking branch of government, such as the Congress of the United States.

Legislature An officially selected body of persons vested with the responsibility and the power to make laws for a political unit, such as a nation.

Letters of marque and reprisal Documents issued by a nation allowing a private citizen to seize citizens or goods of another nation. For example, to allow a private citizen to equip a ship with arms in order to attack enemy ships.

Levy To impose or collect, often a tax.

Logrolling The exchanging of political favors, especially the trading of influence or votes among legislators, to achieve passage of projects of interest to one another.

Magazine A place where goods are stored, especially a building or a storeroom on a warship where ammunition is stored.

Measure A legislative proposed law or enactment.

Militia A military force that is not part of a regular army and is subject to call for service in an emergency.

Minister A person authorized to represent his or her government in diplomatic dealings with other governments, usually ranking immediately below an ambassador.

Misdemeanor An offense of lesser gravity than a felony.

Naturalization The granting of full citizenship to one of foreign birth.

Omnibus bill A legislative bill that includes many various separate and distinct matters, and frequently one joining a number of different subjects in one measure in such a way as to compel the executive authority to accept provisions which he or she does not approve or else defeat the whole enactment.

Ordain To order by virtue of superior authority; decree or enact.

Overt Open and observable; not concealed or hidden

Pardon To release a person from punishment.

Piracies Robberies at sea.

Pocket veto The president's indirect veto of a bill presented to him or her within ten days of Congressional adjournment, by his or her retaining the bill unsigned until Congress adjourns.

Poll tax A tax levied on persons rather than on property, often as a requirement for voting.

Pork (slang) Government funds, appointments, or other favors acquired by a representative for his or her constituency.

Pork barrel (slang) A government project or appropriation benefiting a specific locale and a certain legislator's constituents.

Posterity Future generations.

Preamble A preliminary statement, especially the introduction to a formal document that explains its purpose.

President pro tempore (informally: president pro tem), The senator who presides over the US Senate in the absence of the vice president, who is constitutionally the president of the Senate.

Prosecute To initiate legal or criminal court action against a person or entity.

Provisions Stipulations or qualifications, especially clauses in a document or agreement.

Quartering The British Parliament passed the Quartering Act in 1765. It ordered the colonies to supply the soldiers of the crown with living quarters, fuel, candles, and either cider or beer.

Quorum The minimum number of officers and members of a committee or organization, usually a majority, quorum. Both the House and the Senate require a majority to constitute a quorum.

Ratify To give formal approval and so to make valid.

Redress To set right; remedy or rectify.

Repeal To revoke (withdraw); rescind (make void, annul).

Representative In the United States, a member of the House of Representatives or of a state legislature.

Reprieve The postponement of a punishment.

Republican A person favoring a form of government in which the supreme power lies in a body of citizens who are entitled to vote for officers and representatives responsible to them. (This term was chosen as the name for one of the United States' two major political parties.)

Resolution A formal statement of a decision or expression of opinion put before or adopted by an assembly such as the US Congress.

Revenue The income of a government from all sources appropriated for the payment of the public expenses.

Rider A clause, usually having little relevance to the main issue, added to a legislative bill.

Self-incrimination Incrimination of oneself, especially by one's own testimony in a criminal prosecution.

Second Continental Congress This group met in May 1775 in Philadelphia. Both the Declaration of Independence and the Articles of Confederation were written under the authority of this Continental Congress.

Senate The upper house of the US Congress.

Senator A member of the US Senate.

Speaker In the US Congress, the presiding officer of the House of Representatives.

Suffrage The right or privilege of voting.

Tariff A tax on foreign-made goods entering a country.

Tender (legal tender) Tender comprises all coins and currencies of the United States (including Federal Reserve notes and circulating notes of Federal Reserve banks and national banking associations). Regardless of when they were coined or issued, they are legal tender for all debts, public and private, public charges, taxes, duties, and dues.

Tenure The period of time for which an office holder keeps his or her position.

Testimony A declaration or affirmation of fact or truth, as that given before a court.

Title of Nobility Formal names attached to a person by virtue of office, rank, hereditary privilege, noble birth, or attainment, or as a mark of respect. The colonists would have recognized English titles. Titles for men in descending order are duke, marquis, earl, viscount, and baron. Titles for women in descending order are duchess, marchioness, countess, vice countess, and baroness.

Treason Article III, Section 3 of the US Constitution defines treason against the United States as the act of levying war against them, or in adhering to their enemies or giving them aid and comfort.

Treaty A formal agreement between two or more states.

Tribunals Courts of justice.

Unlawful restraint Preventing a person who has been arrested from being brought before a court.

Vessels Crafts, especially those larger than a rowboat, designed to navigate on water.

Vested Placed in control of something.

Veto The vested power or constitutional right of a chief executive to reject a bill passed by a legislative body and thus prevent or delay its enactment into law.

Warrants Judicial writs (written court orders) authorizing an officer to make a search, seizure, or arrest or to execute a judgment.

Writ of habeas corpus One of a variety of writs (written court orders) having as its function the release of a party from unlawful restraint.

ARTICLES OF CONFEDERATION

To all to whom these presents shall come, we the undersigned delegates of the states affixed to our names, send greeting:

Whereas the delegates of the United States of America in Congress assembled, did, on the fifteenth day of November in the year of our Lord seventeen seventy-seven, and in the second year of the Independence of America, agree to Certain Articles of Confederation and perpetual union between the states of New Hampshire, Massachusetts Bay, Rhode Island and Providence Plantations, Connecticut, New York, New Jersey, Pennsylvania, Delaware, Maryland, Virginia, North Carolina, South Carolina and Georgia in the words following, viz:

Articles of Confederation and Perpetual Union Between the States of New Hampshire, Massachusetts Bay, Rhode Island and Providence Plantations, Connecticut, New York, New Jersey, Pennsylvania, Delaware, Maryland, Virginia, North Carolina, South Carolina and Georgia.

ARTICLE I. The style of this Confederacy shall be "The United States of America."

ARTICLE II. Each state retains its sovereignty, freedom and independence, and every power, jurisdiction and right which is not by this Confederation expressly delegated to the United States in Congress assembled.

ARTICLE III. The said states hereby severally enter into a firm league of friendship with each other for their common defence, the security of their liberties, and their mutual and general welfare, binding themselves to assist each other against all force offered to, or attacks made upon them, or any of them, on account of religion, sovereignty, trade, or any other pretence whatever.

ARTICLE IV. The better to secure and perpetuate mutual friendship and intercourse among the people of the different States in this Union, the free inhabitants of each of these states, paupers, vagabonds and fugitives from justice excepted, shall be entitled to all privileges and immunities of free citizens in the several states; and the people of each state shall have free ingress and regress to and from any other state, and shall enjoy therein all the privileges of trade and commerce, subject to the same duties, impositions and restrictions as the inhabitants thereof respectively; provided, that such restrictions shall not extend so far as to prevent the removal of property imported into any state, to any other state of which the owner is an inhabitant; provided also, that no imposition, duties or restriction shall be laid by any state on the property of the United States, or either of them.

If any person guilty of or charged with treason, felony, or other high misdemeanor in any state, shall flee from justice, and be found in any of the United States, he shall upon demand of the governor or executive power of the state from which he fled, be delivered up and removed to the state having jurisdiction of his offense.

Full faith and credit shall be given in each of these to the records, acts and judicial proceedings of the courts and magistrates of every other state.

ARTICLE V. For the more convenient management of the general interests of the United States, delegates shall be annually appointed in such manner as the legislature of each state shall direct, to meet in Congress on the first Monday in November, in every year, with a power, reserved to each state, to recall its delegates, or any of them, at any time within the year, and to send others in their stead, for the remainder of the year. No state shall be represented in Congress by less than two, nor by more than seven members; and no person shall be capable of being a delegate for more than three years in any term of six years; nor shall any person, being a delegate, be capable of holding any office under the United States, for which he, or another for his benefit receives any salary, fees or emolument of any kind.

Each state shall maintain its own delegates in a meeting of the states, and while they act as members of the committee of the states.

In determining questions in the United States, in Congress assembled, each state shall have one vote.

Freedom of speech and debate in Congress shall not be impeached or questioned in any court, or place out of Congress, and the members of Congress shall be protected in their persons from arrests and imprisonments, during the time of their going to and from, and attendance on Congress, except for treason, felony, or breach of the peace.

ARTICLE VI. No state without the consent of the United States in Congress assembled, shall send any embassy to, or receive any embassy from, or enter into any conference, agreement, alliance or treaty with any king, prince or state; nor shall any person holding any office of profit or trust under the United States, or any of them, accept of any, present, emolument, office or title of any kind whatever from any king, prince or foreign state; nor shall the United States in Congress assembled, or any of them, grant any title of nobility.

No two or more states shall enter into any treaty, confederation or alliance whatever between them, without the consent of the United States in Congress assembled, specifying accurately the purposes for which the same is to be entered into, and how long it shall continue.

No state shall lay any impost or duties, which may interfere with any stipulations in treaties, entered into by the United States in Congress assembled, with any king, prince or state, in pursuance of any treaties already proposed by Congress to the courts of France and Spain.

No vessels of war shall be kept up in time of peace by any state, except such number only as shall be deemed necessary by the United States in Congress assembled, for the defence of such state, or its trade; nor shall any body of forces be kept up by any state, in time of peace except such number only, as in the judgment of the United States, Congress assembled, shall be deemed requisite to garrison the forts necessary for the defence of such state; but every state shall always keep up a well regulated and disciplined militia, sufficiently armed and accoutered, and shall provide and constantly have ready for us, in public stores, a due number of field pieces and tents, and a proper quantity of arms, ammunition and camp equipage.

No state shall engage in any war without the consent of the United States in Congress assembled, unless such state be actually invaded by enemies, or shall have received certain advice of a resolution being formed by some nation of Indians to invade such state, and the danger is so imminent as not to admit of a delay, till the United States in Congress assembled can be consulted: nor shall any state grant commissions to any ships or vessels of war, nor letters of marque or reprisal, except it be after a declaration of war by the United States in Congress assembled, and then only against the kingdom or state and the subjects thereof, against which war has been so declared, and under such regulations as shall be established by the United States in Congress assembled, unless such state be infested by pirates, in which case vessels of war be fitted out for that occasion, and kept so long as the danger shall continue, or until the United States in Congress assembled shall determine otherwise.

ARTICLE VII. When land forces are raised by any state for the common defence, all officers of or under the rank of colonel, shall be appointed by the Legislature of each state respectively by whom such forces shall be raised, or in such manner as such state shall direct, all vacancies shall be filled up by the state which first made the appointment.

ARTICLE VIII. All charges of war, and all other expenses that shall be incurred for the common defence or general welfare, and allowed by the United States in Congress assembled, shall be defrayed out of a common treasury, which shall be supplied by the several states, in proportion to the value of all land within each state, granted to or surveyed for any person, as such land and the buildings and improvements thereon shall be estimated according to such mode as the United States in Congress assembled, shall from time to time direct and appoint.

The taxes for paying that proportion shall be laid and levied by the authority and direction of the legislatures of the several states within the time agreed upon by the United States in Congress assembled.

ARTICLE IX. The United States in Congress assembled, shall have the sole and exclusive right and power of determining on peace and war except in the cases mentioned in the sixth article; of sending and receiving ambassadors; entering into treaties and alliances; provided that no treaty of commerce shall be made whereby the legislative power of the respective states shall be restrained from imposing such imposts and duties on foreigners, as their own people are subjected to, or from prohibiting the exportation or importation of any species of goods or commodities whatsoever; of establishing rules for deciding in all cases, what captures on land or water shall be legal, and in what manner prizes taken by land or naval forces in the service of the United States shall be divided or appropriated; of granting letters of marque and reprisal in times of peace; appointing courts for the trial of piracies and felonies committed on the high seas and establishing courts for receiving and determining finally appeals in all cases of captures, provided that no member of Congress shall be appointed a judge of any of said courts.

The United States in Congress assembled shall also be the last resort on appeal in all disputes and differences now subsisting or that hereafter may arise between two or more states concerning boundary, jurisdiction or any other cause whatever; which authority shall always be exercised in the manner following. Whenever the legislative or executive authority or lawful agent of any state in controversy with another shall present a petition to Congress, stating the matter in question and praying for a hearing, notice thereof shall be given by order of Congress to the legislative or executive authority of the other state in controversy, and a day assigned for the appearance of the parties by their lawful agents, who shall then be directed to appoint by joint consent commissioners or judges to constitute a court for hearing and determining the matter in question: but if they can not agree, Congress shall name three persons out of each of the United States, and from the list of such persons each party shall alternately strike out one, the petitioners beginning, until the number shall be reduced to thirteen; and from that number not less than seven, or more than nine names, as Congress shall direct, shall in the presence of Congress be drawn out by lot, and the persons whose names shall be so drawn or any five of them, shall be commissioners or judges, to hear and finally determine the controversy, so always as a major part of the judges who shall hear the cause shall agree in the determination: and if either party shall neglect to attend at the day appointed, without showing reasons, which Congress judge sufficient, or being present shall refuse to strike, the Congress shall proceed to nominate three persons out of each state, and the Secretary of Congress shall strike in behalf of such party absent or refusing; and the judgment and sentence of the court to be appointed, in the manner before prescribed, shall be final and conclusive; and if any of the parties shall refuse to submit to the authority of such court, or to appear or defend their claim or cause, the court shall, nevertheless proceed to pronounce sentence, or judgment, which shall in like manner be final and decisive, the judgment or sentence and other proceeds being in either case transmitted to Congress, and lodged among the acts of Congress for the security of the parties concerned: provided that every commissioner, before he sits in judgment, shall take an oath to be administered by one of the judges of the supreme or superior court of the state where the cause shall be tried, "well and truly to hear and determine the matter in question, according to the best of his judgment without favor, affection, or hope of reward": provided also that no state shall be deprived of territory for the benefit of the United States.

All controversies concerning the private right of soil claimed under different grants of two or more states, whose jurisdiction as they may respect such lands, and the states which passed such grants are adjusted, the said grants or either of them being at the same time claimed to have originated antecedent to such settlement or jurisdiction, shall on the petition of either party to the Congress of the United States, be finally determined as near as may be in the same manner as is before prescribed for deciding disputes respecting territorial jurisdiction between the different states.

The United States in Congress assembled shall also have the sole and exclusive right and power of regulating the alloy and value of coin struck by their own authority, or by that of respective state fixing the standard of weights and measures throughout the United States regulating the trade, and managing all affairs with the Indians, not members of any of the states, provided that the legislative right of state within its own limits be not infringed or violated; establishing and regulating post offices from one state to another, throughout all the United States, and exacting such postage on the papers passing through the same as may be requisite to defray the expenses of the said office; appointing all officers of the land forces, in the service of the United States, excepting regimental officers; appointing all the officers of the naval forces, and commissioning all officers whatever in the service of the United States; making rules for the government and regulation of said land and naval forces, and directing their operations.

The United States in Congress assembled shall have authority to appoint a committee, to sit in the recess of Congress to be denominated "a Committee of the States," and to consist of one delegate from each state; and to appoint such other committees and civil officers as may be necessary for managing the general affairs of the United States under their direction; to appoint one of their number to preside, provided that no person be allowed to serve in the office of president more than one year in any term of three years; to ascertain the necessary sums of money to be raised for the service of the United States, and to appropriate and apply the same for defraying the public expenses; to borrow money, or emit bills on the credit of the United States, transmitting every half year to the respective states an account of the sums of money so borrowed or emitted; to build and equip a navy; to agree upon the number of land forces, and to make requisitions from each state for its quota, in proportion to the number of white inhabitants in such state; which requisition shall be binding, and thereupon the legislature of each state shall appoint the regimental officers, raise the men and clothe, arm and equip them in a soldier-like manner, at the expense of the United States; and the officers and men so clothed, armed and equipped shall march to the place appointed, and within the time agreed on by the United States in Congress assembled: but if the United States in Congress assembled shall, on consideration of circumstances judge proper that any state should not raise men, or should raise a smaller number than its quota, and that any other state should raise a greater number of men than the quota thereof, such extra number shall be raised, officered, clothed, armed and equipped in the same manner as the quota of such state, unless the legislature of such state shall judge that such extra number can not be safely spared out of the same, in which case they shall raise, officer, clothe, arm and equip as many of such extra number as they judge can be safely spared. And the officers and men so clothed, armed and equipped, shall march to the place appointed, and within the time agreed on by the United States in Congress assembled.

The United States in Congress assembled shall never engage in war, nor grant letters of marque and reprisal in time of peace, nor enter into any treaties or alliances, nor coin money, nor regulate the value thereof, nor ascertain the sums and expenses necessary for the defense and welfare of the United States, or any of them, nor emit bills, nor borrow money on the credit of the United States, nor appropriate money, nor agree upon the number of vessels of war, to be built or purchased, or the number of land or sea forces to be raised, nor appoint a commander-in-chief of the army or navy, unless nine states assent to the same: nor shall a question on any other point, except for adjourning from day to day be determined, unless by the votes of a majority of the United States in Congress assembled.

The Congress of the United States shall have power to adjourn to any time within the year, and to any place within the United States. so that no period of adjournment be for a longer duration than the space of six months; and shall publish the journal of their proceedings monthly, except such parts thereof relating to treaties, alliances or military operations, as in their judgment require secrecy; and the yeas and nays of the delegates of each state on any question shall be entered on the journal, when it is desired by any delegate; and the delegates of a state, or any of them, at his or their request, shall be furnished with transcript of the said journal, except such parts as are above excepted to lay before the legislatures of the several states.

ARTICLE X. The Committee of the States, or any nine of them shall be authorized to execute, in the recess of Congress, such of the powers of Congress as the United States in Congress assembled, by the consent of nine states, shall from time to time think expedient to vest them with; provided that no power be delegated to the said committee for the exercise of which, by the Articles of Confederation, the voice of nine states in the Congress of the United States assembled is requisite.

ARTICLE XI. Canada acceding to this Confederation, and joining in the measures of the United States, shall be admitted into, and entitled to all the advantages of this Union: but no other colony shall be admitted into the same, unless such admission be agreed to by nine states.

ARTICLE XII. All bills of credit emitted, moneys borrowed and debts contracted by, or under the authority of Congress, before the assembling of the United States, in pursuance of the present

Confederation, shall be deemed and considered as a charge against the United States, for payment and satisfaction whereof the said United States and the public faith are hereby solemnly pledged.

ARTICLE XIII. Every state shall abide by the determinations of the United States in Congress assembled, on all questions which by this Confederation are submitted to them. And the Articles of this Confederation shall be inviolably observed by every state, and the Union shall be perpetual; nor shall any alteration at any time hereafter be made in any of them, unless such alteration be agreed to in a Congress of the United States, and be afterwards confirmed by the legislatures of every state.

AND WHEREAS it hath pleased the Great Governor of the World to incline the hearts of the legislatures we respectively represent in Congress, to approve of, and to authorize us to ratify the said Articles of Confederation and perpetual Union. Know ye that we the undersigned delegates, by virtue of the power and authority to us given for that purpose, do by these presents, in the name and in behalf of our respective constituents, fully and entirely ratify and confirm each and every of the said Articles of Confederation and perpetual Union, and all the singular the matters and things therein contained: and we do further solemnly plight and engage the faith of our respective constituents, that they shall abide by the determinations of the United States Congress assembled, on all questions, which by the said Confederation are submitted to them. And that the articles thereof shall be inviolably observed by the states we respectively represent, and that the Union shall be perpetual.

IN WITNESS WHEREOF we have hereunto set our hands in Congress. Done at Philadelphia in the State of Pennsylvania the ninth day of July in the year of our Lord one thousand seven hundred and seventy-eight, and in the third year of the independence of America.

On the part and behalf of New Hampshire.
> Josiah Bartlett
> John Wentworth, Junr. August 8th, 1778

On the part and behalf of the State of Massachusetts Bay.
> John Hancock
> James Lovell
> Francis Dana
> Elbridge Gerry
> Samuel Adams
> Samuel Holton

On the part and behalf of Rhode Island and Providence Plantations.

> William Ellery
> John Collins
> Henry Marchant

On the part and behalf of the State of Connecticut.
> Roger Sherman
> Andrew Adams
> Titus Hosmer
> Oliver Wolcott
> Samuel Huntington

On the part and behalf of the State of New York.
    Jas. Duane
    Gouv. Morris
    Wm. Duer
    Fra. Lewis

On the part and behalf of the State of New Jersey (Novr. 26, 1778.)
    Jno. Witherspoon
    Nathl. Scudder

On the part and behalf of the State of Pennsylvania.
    Robt. Moqis
    Joseph Reed
    William Clingan
    Jona. Bayard Smith
    Daniael Roberdeau 22d July 1778

On the part of behalf of the State of Delaware.
    Tho. M'Kean
    John Dickinson
    Nicholas VanDyke Feby. 12, 1779 May 5th, 1779

On the part and behalf of the State of Maryland.
    John Hanson
    Daniel Carroll March 1, 1781

On the part and behalf of the State of Virginia.
    Richard Henry Lee
    Jno. Harvie
    John Banister
    Francis Lightfoot Lee
    Thomas Adams

On the part and behalf of the State of North Carolina.
    John Penn
    Conms. Harnett
    Jno. Williams July 21 st, 1778

On the part and behalf of the State of South Carolina.
    Henry Laurens
    Thos. Heyward Junr.
    'Richd. Hutson
    William Henry Drayton
    Jno. Mathews

On the part and behalf of the State of Georgia.
    Jno. Walton
    Edwd. Langworthy
    Edwd. Telfair 24th July, 1778

The Original, Unamended Constitution

PREAMBLE

We, the people of the United States, in order to form a more perfect Union, establish justice, insure domestic tranquility, provide for the common defense, promote the general welfare, and secure the blessings of liberty to ourselves and our posterity, do ordain and establish this Constitution for the United States of America.

ARTICLE I

Section 1. **Legislative powers; in whom vested**

All legislative powers herein granted shall be vested in a Congress of the United States, which shall consist of a Senate and House of Representatives.

Section 2. **House of Representatives, how and by whom chosen Qualifications of a Representative. Representatives and direct taxes, how apportioned. Enumeration. Vacancies to be filled. Power of choosing officers, and of impeachment.**

1. The House of Representatives shall be composed of members chosen every second year by the people of the several States, and the elector in each State shall have the qualifications requisite for electors of the most numerous branch of the State Legislature.

2. No person shall be a Representative who shall not have attained the age of twenty-five years, and been seven years a citizen of the United States, and who shall not, when elected, be an inhabitant of that State in which he shall be chosen.

3. Representatives [and direct taxes] {Altered by 16th Amendment} shall be apportioned among the several States which may be included within this Union, according to their respective numbers, [which shall be determined by adding the whole number of free persons, including those bound to service for a term of years, and excluding Indians not taxed, three-fifth of all other persons.] {Altered by 14th Amendment} The actual enumeration shall be made within three years after the first meeting of the Congress of the United States, and within every subsequent term often years, in such manner as they shall by law direct. The number of Representatives shall not exceed one for every thirty thousand, but each State shall have at least one Representative; and until such enumeration shall be made, the State of New Hampshire shall be entitled to choose three, Massachusetts eight, Rhode Island and Providence Plantations one, Connecticut five, New York six, New Jersey four, Pennsylvania eight, Delaware one, Maryland six, Virginia ten, North Carolina five, South Carolina five, and Georgia three.

4. When vacancies happen in the representation from any State, the Executive Authority thereof shall issue writs of election to fill such vacancies.

5. The House of Representatives shall choose their Speaker and other officers; and shall have the sole power of impeachment.

Section 3. **Senators, how and by whom chosen. How classified. State Executive, when to make temporary appointments, in case, etc. Qualifications of a Senator. President of the Senate, his right to vote. President pro tem., and other officers of the Senate, how chosen. Power to try impeachments. When President is tried, Chief Justice to preside. Sentence.**

1. The Senate of the United States shall be composed of two Senators from each State, [chosen by the Legislature thereof,] {Altered by 17th Amendment} for six years; and each Senator shall have one vote.

2. Immediately after they shall be assembled in consequence of the first election, they shall be divided as equally as may be into three classes. The seats of the Senators of the first class shall be vacated at the expiration of the second year, of the second class at the expiration of the fourth year, and of the third class at the expiration of the sixth year, so that one-third may be chosen every second year; [and if vacancies happen by resignation, or otherwise, during the recess of the Legislature of any State, the Executive thereof may make temporary appointments until the next meeting of the Legislature, which shall then fill such vacancies.] {Altered by 17th Amendment}

3. No person shall be a Senator who shall not have attained to the age of thirty years, and been nine years a citizen of the United States, and who shall not, when elected, be an inhabitant of that State for which he shall be chosen.

4. The Vice-President of the United States shall be President of the Senate, but shall have no vote, unless they be equally divided.

5. The Senate shall choose their other officers, and also a President pro tempore, in the absence of the Vice President, or when he shall exercise the office of the President of the United States.

6. The Senate shall have the sole power to try all impeachments. When sitting for that purpose, they shall be an oath of affirmation. When the President of the United States is tried, the Chief Justice shall preside: and no person shall be convicted without the concurrence of two-thirds of the members present.

7. Judgment in cases of impeachment shall not extend further than to removal from office, and disqualification to hold and enjoy any office of honor, trust, or profit under the United States: but the party convicted shall nevertheless be liable and subject to indictment, trial, judgment and punishment, according to law.

Section 4.   **Times, etc., of holding elections, how prescribed. One session in each year.**

1. The times, places and manner of holding elections for Senators and Representatives, shall be prescribed in each State by the Legislature thereof; but the Congress may at any time by law make or alter such regulations, except as to the places of choosing Senators.

2. The Congress shall assemble at least once in every year, and such meeting shall be [on the first Monday in December,] {Altered by 20th Amendment} unless they by law appoint a different day.

Section 5.   **Membership, Quorum, Adjournments, Rules, Power to punish or expel. Journal. Time of adjournments, how limited etc.**

1. Each House shall be the judge of the elections, returns and qualifications of its own members, and a majority of each shall constitute a quorum to do business; but a smaller number may adjourn from day to day, and may be authorized to compel the attendance of absent members, in such manner, and under such penalties as each House may provide.

2. Each House may determine the rules of its proceedings, punish its members for disorderly behavior, and, with the concurrence of two-thirds, expel a member.

3. Each House shall keep a journal of its proceedings, and from time to time publish the same, expecting such parts as may in their judgment require secrecy; and the yeas and nays of the members of either House on any question shall, at the desire of one-fifth of those present, be entered on the journal.

4. Neither House, during the session of Congress, shall, without the consent of the other, adjourn for more than three days, nor to any other place than that in which the two Houses shall be sitting.

Section 6.   **Compensation, Privileges, Disqualification in certain cases.**

1. The Senators and Representatives shall receive a compensation for their services, to be ascertained by law, and paid out of the Treasury of the United States. They shall in all cases, except treason, felony and breach of the peace, be privileged from arrest during their attendance at the session of their respective Houses, and in going to and returning from the same; and for any speech or debate in either House, they shall not be questioned in any other place.

2. No Senator or Representative shall, during the time for which he was elected, be appointed to any civil office under the authority of the United States, which shall have increased during such time; and no person holding any office under the United States, shall be a member of either House during his continuance in office.

Section 7. **House to originate all revenue bills. Veto. Bill may be passed by two-thirds of each House, notwithstanding, etc. Bill, not returned in ten days to become a law. .Provisions as to orders, concurrent resolutions, etc.**

1. All bills for raising revenue shall originate in the House of Representatives; but the Senate may propose or concur with amendments as on other bills.

2. Every bill which shall have passed the House of Representatives and the Senate, shall, before it become a law, be presented to the president of the United States; if he approve, he shall sign it, but if not, he shall return it, with his objections, to that house in which it shall have originated, who shall enter the objections at large on their journal, and proceed to reconsider it. If after such reconsideration, two thirds of that house shall agree to pass the bill, it shall be sent, together with the objections, to the other house, by which it shall likewise be reconsidered, and if approved by two-thirds of that house it shall become a law. But in all such cases the votes of both houses shall be determined by yeas and nays, and the names of the persons voting for and against the bill shall be entered on the journal of each house respectively. If any bill shall not be returned by the president within ten days (Sundays excepted) after it shall have been presented to him, the same shall be a law, in like manner as if he had signed it, unless the Congress by their adjournment prevent its return, in which case it shall not be a law.

3. Every order, resolution, or vote to which the concurrence of the Senate and House of Representatives may be necessary (except on a question of adjournment) shall be presented to the president of the United States; and before the same shall take effect, shall be approved by him, or, being disapproved by him, shall be re-passed by two-thirds of the Senate and House of Representatives, according to the rules and limitations prescribed in the case of a bill.

Section 8. **Powers of Congress**

The Congress shall have the power

1. To lay and collect taxes, duties, imposts and excises, to pay the debts and provide for the common defence and general welfare of the United States; but all duties, imposts and excises shall be uniform throughout the United States;

2. To borrow money on the credit of the United States;

3. To regulate commerce with foreign nations, and among the several states, and with the Indian tribes;

4. To establish an uniform rule of naturalization, and uniform laws on the subject of bankruptcies throughout the United States;

5. To coin money, regulate the value thereof, and of foreign coin, and fix the standard of weights and measures;

6. To provide for the punishment of counterfeiting the securities and current coin of the United States;

7. To establish post-offices and post-roads;

8. To promote the progress of science and useful arts, by securing for limited times to authors and inventors the exclusive right to their respective writings and discoveries;

9. To constitute tribunals inferior to the supreme court;

10. To define and punish piracies and felonies committed on the high seas, and offences against the law of nations;

11. To declare war, grant letters of marque and reprisal, and make rules concerning captures on land and water;

12. To raise and support armies, but no appropriation of money to that use shall be for a longer term than two years;

13. To provide and maintain a navy;

14. To make rules for the government and regulation of the land and naval forces;

15. To provide for calling forth the militia to execute the laws of the union, suppress insurrections and repel invasions;

16. To provide for organizing, arming and disciplining the militia, and for governing such part of them as may be employed in the service of the United States, reserving to the states respectively, the appointment of the officers, and the authority of training the militia according to the discipline prescribed by Congress;

17. To exercise exclusive legislation in all cases whatsoever, over such district (not exceeding ten miles square) as may, by cession of particular states, and the acceptance of Congress, become the seat of the government of the United States, and to exercise like authority over all places purchased by the consent of the legislature of the state in which the same shall be, for the erection of forts, magazines, arsenals, dock-yards, and other needful buildings;

And, 18. To make all laws which shall be necessary and proper for carrying into execution the foregoing powers, and all other powers vested by this constitution in the government of the United States, or in any department or officer thereof.

Section 9.   **Provision as to migration or importation of certain persons. Habeas Corpus, Bills of attainder, etc. Taxes, how apportioned. No export duty. No commercial preference. Money, how drawn from Treasury, etc. No titular nobility. Officers not to receive presents, etc.**

1. The migration or importation of such persons as any of the states now existing shall think proper to admit, shall not be prohibited by the Congress prior to the year 1808, but a tax or duty may be imposed on such importations, not exceeding 10 dollars for each person.

2. The privilege of the writ of habeas corpus shall not be suspended, unless when in cases of rebellion or invasion the public safety may require it.

3. No bill of attainder or ex post facto law shall be passed.

4.   [No capitation, or other direct tax shall be laid unless in proportion to the census or enumeration herein before direction to be taken.] {Altered by 16th Amendment}

4. No tax or duty shall be laid on articles exported from any state.

5. No preference shall be given by any regulation of commerce or revenue to the ports of one state over those of another: nor shall vessels bound to, or from one state, be obliged to enter, clear, or pay duties in another.

6. No money shall be drawn from the treasury but in consequence of appropriations made by law; and a regular statement and account of the receipts and expenditures of all public money shall be published from time to time.

7. No title of nobility shall be granted by the United States: And no person holding any office or profit or trust under them, shall, without the consent of the Congress, accept of any present, emolument, office, or title, or any kind whatever, from any king, prince, or foreign state.

Section 10.   **States prohibited from the exercise of certain powers.**

1. No state shall enter into any treaty, alliance, or confederation; grant letters of marque and reprisal; coin money; emit bills of credit; make any thing but gold and silver coin a tender in payment of debts; pass any bill of attainder, ex post facto law, or law impairing the obligation of contracts, or grant any title of nobility.

2. No state shall, without the consent of the Congress, lay any imposts or duties on imports or exports, except what may be absolutely necessary for executing its inspection laws; and the net produce of all duties and imposts, laid by any state on imports or exports, shall be for the use of the treasury of the United States; and all such laws shall be subject to the revision and control of the Congress.

3. No state shall, without the consent of Congress, lay any duty of tonnage, keep troops, or ships of war in time of peace, enter into any agreement or compact with another state, or with a foreign power, or engage in a war, unless actually invaded, or in such imminent danger as will not admit of delay.

ARTICLE II

Section 1:   **President: his term of office. Electors of President; number and how appointed. Electors to vote on same day. Qualification of President. On whom his duties devolve in case of his removal, death, etc. President's compensation. his oath of office.**

1. The Executive power shall be vested in a President of the United States of America. He shall hold office during the term of four years, and together with the Vice President, chosen for the same term, be elected as follows.

2. [Each state] {Altered by 23rd Amendment} shall appoint, in such manner as the Legislature may direct, a number of electors, equal to the whole number of Senators and Representatives to which the State may be entitled in the Congress: but no Senator or Representative, or person holding an office of trust or profit under the United States, shall be appointed an elector [The electors shall meet in their respective States, and vote by ballot for two persons, of whom one at least shall not be an inhabitant of the same State with themselves. And they shall make a list of all the persons voted for each; which list to the President of the Senate. The President of the Senate shall, in the presence of the Senate and House of Representatives, open all the certificates, and the votes shall then be counted. The person having the greatest number of votes shall be the President, if such number be a majority of the whole number of electors appointed; and if there be more than one who have such majority, and have an equal number of votes, then the House of Representatives shall immediately choose by ballot one of them for President; and if no person have a majority, then from the five highest on the list the said House shall in like manner choose the President. But in choosing the President, the votes shall be taken by States, the representation from each State having one vote; a quorum for this purpose shall consist of a member or members from two-thirds of the States, and a majority of all the States shall be necessary to a choice. In every case, after the choice of the President, the person having the greatest number of votes of the electors shall be the Vice President. But if there should remain two or more who have equal votes, the Senate shall choose from them by ballot the Vice President.] {Altered by 12th Amendment}

3. The Congress may determine the time of choosing the electors, and the day on which they shall give their votes; which day shall be the same throughout the United States.

4. No person except a natural born citizen, or a citizen of the United States, at the time of the adoption of this Constitution, shall be eligible to the office of President; neither shall any person be eligible to that office who shall not have attained to the age of thirty-five years, and been fourteen years a resident within the United States.

5. [In case of the removal of the President from office, or of his death, resignation, or inability to discharge the powers and duties of the said office, the same shall devolve on the Vice President, and the Congress may by law provide for the case of removal, death, resignation, or inability, both of the President and Vice President, declaring what officer shall then act as President, and such officer shall act accordingly, until the disability be removed, or a President shall be elected.] {Altered by 25th Amendment}

6. The President shall, at stated times, receive for his services, a compensation, which shall neither be increased nor diminished during the period for which he shall have been elected, and he shall not receive within that period any other emolument from the United States, or any of them.

7. Before he enter on the execution of his office, he shall take the following oath or affirmation: "I do solemnly swear (or affirm) that I will faithfully execute the office of the President of the United States, and will to the best of my ability, preserve, protect and defend the Constitution of the United States."

Section 2.   **President to be Commander-in-Chief. He may require opinions of cabinet officers, etc., may pardon. Treaty-making power. Nomination of certain officers. When President may fill vacancies.**

1. The President shall be Commander-in-Chief of the Army and Navy of the United States, and of the militia of the several States, when called into the actual service of the United States; he may require the opinion, in writing, of the principal officer in each of the executive departments, upon any subject relating to the duties of their respective offices, and he shall have power to grant reprieves and pardons for offenses against the United States, except in cases of impeachment.

2. He shall have power, by and with the advice and consent of the Senate, to make treaties, provided two-thirds of the Senators present concur; and he shall nominate, and by and with the advice and consent of the Senate, shall appoint ambassadors, other public ministers and consuls, judges of the Supreme Court, and all other officers of the United States, whose appointments are not herein otherwise provided for, and which shall be established by law: but the Congress may by law vest the appointment of such inferior officers, as they think proper, in the President alone, in the courts of law, or in the heads of departments.

3. The President shall have the power to fill up all vacancies that may happen during the recess of the Senate, by granting commissions, which shall expire at the end of their next session.

Section 3.   **President shall communicate to Congress. He may convene and adjourn Congress, in case of disagreement, etc. Shall receive ambassadors, execute laws, and commission officers.**

He shall from time to time give to the Congress information of the state of the Union, and recommend to their consideration such measures as he shall judge necessary and expedient; he may, on extraordinary occasions, convene both Houses, or either of them, and in case of disagreement between them, with respect to the time of adjournment, he may adjourn them to such time as he shall think proper; he may receive ambassadors, and other public ministers; he shall take care that the laws be faithfully executed, and shall commission all the officers of the United States.

Section 4.   All civil offices forfeited for certain crimes.

The President, Vice President, and all civil officers of the United States, shall be removed from office on impeachment for, and conviction of, treason, bribery, or other high crimes and misdemeanors.

ARTICLE III

Section 1.   Judicial powers. Tenure. Compensation.

The judicial power of the United States, shall be vested in one supreme court, and in such inferior courts as the Congress may, from time to time, ordain and establish. The judges, both of the supreme and inferior courts, shall hold their offices during good behaviour, and shall, at stated times, receive for their services a compensation, which shall not be diminished during their continuance in office.

Section 2.   Judicial power; to what cases it extends. Original jurisdiction of Supreme Court Appellate. Trial by Jury, etc. Trial, where

1. The judicial power shall extend to all cases, in law and equity, arising under this constitution, the laws of the United States, and treaties made, or which shall be made under their authority; to all cases affecting ambassadors, other public ministers and consuls; to all cases of admiralty and maritime jurisdiction; to controversies to which the United States shall be a party; [to controversies between two or more states, between a state and citizens of another state, between citizens of different states, between citizens of the same state, claiming lands under grants of different states, and between a state, or the citizens thereof, and foreign states, citizens or subjects.] {Altered by **11**th Amendment}

2. In all cases affecting ambassadors, other public ministers and consuls, and those in which a state shall be a party, the supreme court shall have original jurisdiction. In all the other cases before-mentioned, the supreme court shall have appellate jurisdiction, both as to law and fact, with such exceptions, and under such regulations as the congress shall make.

3. The trial of all crimes, except in cases of impeachment, shall be by jury; and such trial shall be held in the state where the said crimes shall have been committed; but when not committed within any state, the trial shall be at such place or places as the Congress may by law have directed.

Section 3.   Treason defined. Proof of. Punishment

1. Treason against the United States shall consist only in levying war against them, or in adhering to their enemies, giving them aid and comfort. No person shall be convicted of

treason unless on the testimony of two witnesses to the same overt act, or on confession in open court.

2. The Congress shall have power to declare the punishment of treason, but no attainder of treason shall work corruption of blood, or forfeiture, except during the life of the person attainted.

ARTICLE IV

Section 1.   Each state to give credit to the public acts, etc. of every other State.

Full faith and credit shall be given in each state to the public acts, records and judicial proceedings of every other state. And the Congress may by general laws prescribe the manner in which such acts, records and proceedings shall be proved, and the effect thereof.

Section 2.   Privileges of citizens of each State. Fugitives from Justice to be delivered up. Persons held to service having escaped, to be delivered up.

1. The citizens of each state shall be entitled to all privileges and immunities of citizens in the several states. {See the 14th Amendment}

2. A person charged in any state with treason, felony, or other crime, who shall flee justice, and be found in another state, shall, on demand of the executive authority of the state from which he fled, be delivered up, to be removed to the state having jurisdiction of the crime.

3. [No person held to service or labour in one state, under the laws thereof, escaping into another, shall in consequence of any law or regulation therein, be discharged from such service or labour, but shall be delivered up on claim of the party to whom such service or labour may be due.] {Altered by 13th Amendment}

Section 3.   Admission of new States. Power of Congress over territory and other property.

1. New states may be admitted by the Congress into this union; but no new state shall be formed or erected within the jurisdiction of any other state, nor any state be formed by the junction of two or more states, without the consent of the legislatures of the states concerned, as well as of the Congress.

2. The Congress shall have power to dispose of and make all needful rules and regulations respecting the territory or other property belonging to the United States; and nothing in this constitution shall be so construed as to prejudice any claims of the United States, or of any particular state.

Section 4.   Republican form of government guaranteed. Each State to be protected.

The United States shall guarantee to every state in this union, a republican form of government, and shall protect each of them against invasion; and on application of the legislature, or of the executive (when the legislature cannot be convened), against domestic violence.

ARTICLE V

Amendments

The Congress, whenever two-thirds of both houses shall deem it necessary, shall propose amendments to this constitution, or on the application of the legislatures of two-thirds of the several states, shall call a convention for proposing amendments, which, in either case, shall be valid to all intents and purposes, as part of this constitution, when ratified by the legislatures of three-fourths of the several states, or by conventions in three-fourths thereof, as the one or the other mode of ratification may be proposed by the Congress: Provided, that no amendment which may be made prior to the year 1808, shall in any manner affect the first and fourth clauses in the ninth section of the first article; and that no state, without its consent, shall be deprived of its equal suffrage in the Senate.

ARTICLE VI

1. All debts contracted and engagements entered into, before the adoption of this constitution, shall be as valid against the United States under this constitution, as under the confederation.

2. This constitution, and the laws of the United States which shall be made in pursuance thereof; and all treaties made, or which shall be made, under the authority of the United States shall be the supreme law of the land; and the judges in every state shall be bound thereby, any thing in the constitution or laws of any state to the contrary notwithstanding.

3. The senators and representatives before-mentioned, and the members of the several state legislatures, and all executive and judicial officers, both of the United States and of the several states, shall be bound by oath or affirmation, to support this constitution; but no religious test shall ever be required as a qualification to any office or public trust under the United States.

ARTICLE VII

The ratification of the conventions of nine states, shall be sufficient for the establishment of this constitution between the states so ratifying the same.

The Ten Original Amendments: The Bill of Rights

Passed by Congress September 25, 1789. Ratified December 15, 1792.

AMENDMENT 1

Congress shall make no law respecting an establishment of religion, or prohibiting the free exercise thereof; or abridging the freedom of speech, or of the press; or the right of the people peaceably to assemble, and to petition the Government for a redress of grievances.

AMENDMENT II

A well-regulated militia, being necessary to the security of a free State, the right of the people to keep and bear arms, shall not be infringed.

AMENDMENT III

No soldier shall, in time of peace be quartered in any house, without the consent of the owner, nor in time of war, but in a manner to be prescribed by law.

AMENDMENT IV

The right of the people to be secure in their persons, houses, papers, and effects, against unreasonable searches and seizures, shall not be violated, and no warrants shall issue, but upon probable cause, supported by oath or affirmation, and particularly describing the place to be searched, and the persons or things to be seized.

AMENDMENT V

No person shall be held to answer for a capital, or otherwise infamous crime, unless on a presentment or indictment of a Grand Jury, except in cases arising in the land or naval forces, or in the militia, when in actual service in time of war or public danger; nor shall any person be subject for the same offense to be twice put in jeopardy of life or limb; nor shall be compelled in any criminal case to be a witness against himself, nor be deprived of life, liberty, or property, without due process of law; nor shall private property be taken for public use without just compensation.

AMENDMENT VI

In all criminal prosecutions, the accused shall enjoy the right to a speedy and public trial, by an impartial jury of the State and district wherein the crime shall have been committed, which district shall have been previously ascertained by law, and to be informed of the nature and cause of the accusation; to be confronted with the witnesses against him; to have compulsory process for obtaining witnesses in his favor, and to have the assistance of counsel for his defense.

AMENDMENT VII

In suits at common law, where the value in controversy shall exceed twenty dollars, the right of trial by jury shall be preserved, and no fact tried by a jury shall be otherwise reexamined in any court of the United States, than according to the rules of the common law.

AMENDMENT VIII

Excessive bail shall not be required, nor excessive fines imposed, nor cruel and unusual punishments inflicted.

AMENDMENT IX

The enumeration in the Constitution, of certain rights, shall not be construed to deny or disparage others retained by the people.

AMENDMENT X

The powers not delegated to the United States by the Constitution, nor prohibited by it to the States, are reserved to the States respectively, or to the people.

Amendments XI through XXVII

AMENDMENT XI

Passed by Congress March 4, 1794. Ratified February 7, 1795.

The judicial power of the United States shall not be construed to extend to any suit in law or equity, commenced or prosecuted against one of the United States by citizens of another State, or by citizens or subjects of any foreign state.

AMENDMENT XII

Passed by Congress December 9, 1803. Ratified July 27, 1804.

The Electors shall meet in their respective States and vote by ballot for President and Vice-President, one of whom, at least, shall not be an inhabitant of the same State with themselves; they shall name in their ballots the person voted for as President, and in distinct ballots the person voted for as Vice-President, and of the number of votes for each, which lists they shall sign and certify, and transmit sealed to the seat of the Government of the United States, directed to the President of the Senate; the President of the Senate shall, in the presence of the Senate and House of Representatives, open all the certificates and the votes shall then be counter;- the person having the greatest number of votes for President, shall be the President, if such number be a majority of the whole number of Electors appointed; and if no person have such majority, then from the person shaving the highest numbers not exceeding three on the list of those voted for as President, the House of Representatives shall choose immediately, by ballot, the President. But in choosing the President, the votes shall be taken by States, the representation from each Sate having one vote; a quorum for this purpose shall consist of a member of members from two-thirds of the States, and a majority of all the States shall be necessary to a choice. And if the House of Representatives shall not choose a President whenever the right of choice shall devolve upon them, [before the fourth day of March next following,] {Altered by 20th Amendment} then the Vice-President shall act as President, as in case of the death or other constitutional disability of the President. The person having the greatest number of votes as Vice-President, shall be the Vice-President, if such numbers be a majority of the whole number of electors appointed, and if no person have a majority, then from the two highest numbers on the list, the Senate shall choose the Vice-President; a quorum for the purpose shall consist of two-thirds of the whole number of Senators, and a majority of the whole number shall be necessary to a choice. But no person constitutionally ineligible to the office of President shall be eligible to that of Vice-President of the United States.

AMENDMENT XIII

Passed by Congress January 31, 1865. Ratified December 6, 1865.

Section 1.

Neither slavery nor involuntary servitude, except as a punishment for crime whereof the party shall have been duly convicted, shall exist within the United States, or any place subject to their jurisdiction.

Section 2.

Congress shall have power to enforce this article by appropriate legislation.

AMENDMENT XIV

Passed by Congress June 13, 1866. Ratified July 9, 1868

Section 1.

All persons born or naturalized in the United States, and subject to the jurisdiction thereof, are citizens of the United States and of the State wherein they reside. No State shall make or enforce any law which shall abridge the privileges or immunities of citizens of the United States; nor shall any State deprive any person of life, liberty, or property, without due process of law; nor to deny to any person within its jurisdiction the equal protection of the laws.

Section 2.

Representatives shall be apportioned among the several States according to their respective numbers, counting the whole number of persons in each State, excluding Indians not taxed. But when the right to vote at any election for the choice of Electors for President and Vice-President of the United States, Representatives in Congress, the executive and judicial officers of a State, or the members of the Legislature thereof, is denied to any of the male inhabitants of such State, being twenty-one years of age, and citizens of the United States, or in any way abridged, except for participation in rebellion, or other crime, the basis of representation therein shall be reduced in the proportion which the number of such male citizens shall bear to the whole number of male citizens twenty-one years of age in such State.

Section 3.

No person shall be a Senator or Representative in Congress, or Elector of President and Vice-President, or hold any office, civil or military, under the United States, or under any State, who, having previously taken an oath, as a member of Congress, or as an officer of the United States, or as a member of any State Legislature, or as an executive or judicial officer of any State, to support the Constitution of the Untied States, shall have engaged in insurrection or rebellion against the same, or given aid or comfort to the enemies thereof. But Congress may by a vote of two-thirds of each House, remove such disability.

Section 4.

The validity of the public debt of the United States, authorized by law, including debts incurred for payment of pensions and bounties for services in suppressing insurrection or rebellion, shall not be questioned. But neither the United States nor any State shall assume or pay any debt or obligation incurred in aid of insurrection or rebellion against the United States, or any claim for the loss or emancipation of any slave; but all such debts, obligations and claims shall be held illegal and void.

Section 5.

The Congress shall have the power to enforce, by appropriate legislation, the provisions of this article.

AMENDMENT XV

Passed by Congress February 26, 1869. Ratified February 3, 1870.

Section 1.

The right of citizens of the United States to vote shall not be denied or abridged by the United States or any State on account of race, color, or previous condition of servitude.

Section 2.

The Congress shall have the power to enforce this article by appropriate legislation.

AMENDMENT XVI

Passed by Congress July 2, 1909. Ratified February 3, 1913.

The Congress shall have power to lay and collect taxes on incomes, from whatever sources derived, without apportionment among the several States, and without regard to any census or enumeration.

AMENDMENT XVII

Passed by Congress May 13, 1912. Ratified April 8, 1913.

The Senate of the United States shall be composed of two Senators from each State, elected by the people thereof, for six years; and each Senator shall have one vote. The electors in each State shall have the qualifications requisite for electors of the most numerous branch of the State Legislatures. When vacancies happen in the representation of any State in the Senate, the executive authority of such State shall issue writs of election to fill such vacancies: Provided, That the Legislature of any State may empower the Executive thereof to make temporary appointments until the people fill the vacancies by election as the Legislature may direct. This amendment shall not be so construed as to affect the election or term of any Senator chosen before it becomes valid as part of the Constitution.

AMENDMENT XVIII

Passed by Congress December 18, 1917. Ratified January 16, 1919. {Altered by Amendment 21}

After one year from the ratification of this article the manufacture, sale, or transportation of intoxicating liquors within, the importation thereof into, or the exportation thereof from the Untied States and all territory subject to the jurisdiction thereof for beverage purposes is hereby prohibited. The Congress and the several States shall have concurrent power to enforce this article by appropriate legislation. This article shall be inoperative unless it shall have been ratified as an amendment to the Constitution by the Legislatures of the several States, as provided in the Constitution, within seven years from the date of the submission thereof to the States by the Congress.

AMENDMENT IXX

Passed by Congress June 4, 1919. Ratified August 18, 1920.

The right of citizens of the United States to vote shall not be denied or abridged by the United States or by any State on account of sex. Congress shall have power to enforce this article by appropriate legislation.

AMENDMENT XX

Section 1.

The terms of the President and the Vice-President shall end at noon on the 20th day of January, and the terms of Senators and Representatives at noon on the 3rd day of January, of the years in which such terms would have ended if this article had not been ratified; and the terms of their successors shall then begin.

Section 2.

The Congress shall assemble at least once in every year, and such meeting shall begin at noon on the 3rd day of January, unless they shall by law appoint a different day.

Section 3.

If, at the time fixed for the beginning of the term of the President, the President elect shall have died, the Vice-President elect shall become President. If a President shall not have been chosen before the time fixed for the beginning of his term, or if the President elect shall have failed to qualify, then the Vice-President elect shall act as President until a President shall have qualified; and the Congress may by law provide for the case wherein neither a President elect nor a Vice-President shall have qualified, declaring who shall then act as president, or the manner in which one who is to act shall be selected, and such person shall act accordingly until a President or Vice-President shall have qualified.

Section 4.

The Congress may by law provide for the case of the death of any of the persons from whom the House of representatives may choose a President whenever the right of choice shall have devolved upon them, and for the case of the death of any of the persons form whom the Senate may choose a Vice-President whenever the right of choice shall have devolved upon them.

Section 5.

Sections 1 and 2 shall take effect on the 15th day of October following the ratification of this article (October 1933).

Section 6.

This article shall be inoperative unless it shall have been ratified as an amendment to the Constitution by the Legislatures of three-fourths of the several States within seven years from the date of its submission.

AMENDMENT XXI

Passed by Congress February 20, 1933. Ratified December 5, 1933.

Section 1.

The Eighteenth article of amendment to the Constitution of the United States is hereby repealed.

Section 2.

The transportation or importation into any State, Territory, or Possession of the United States for delivery or use therein of intoxicating liquors, in violation of the laws thereof, is hereby prohibited.

Section 3.

This article shall be inoperative unless it shall have been ratified as an amendment to the Constitution by conventions in the several States, as provided in the Constitution, within seven years from the date of the submission hereof to the States by the Congress.

AMENDMENT XXII

Passed by Congress March 21, 1947. Ratified February 27, 1951.

Section 1.

No person shall be elected to the office of the President more than twice, and no person who has held the office of President, or acted as president, for more than two years of a term to which some other person was elected President shall be elected to the office of President more than once. But this Article shall not apply to any person holding the office of President when this Article was proposed by Congress, and shall not prevent any person who may be holding the office of President, or acting as President, during the term within which this Article becomes operative from holding the office of President or acting as President during the remainder of such term.

Section 2.

This article shall be inoperative unless it shall have been ratified as an amendment to the Constitution by the Legislatures of three-fourths of the several States within seven years from the date of its submission to the States by the Congress.

AMENDMENT XXIII

Passed by Congress June 16, 1960. Ratified March29, 1961.

Section 1.

The District constituting the seat of Government of the United States shall appoint in such manner of Congress may direct: A number of electors of President and Vice President equal to the whole number of Senators and Representatives in Congress to which the District would be entitled if it were a State, but in no event more than the least populous State; they shall be in addition to those appointed by the States, but they shall be considered, for the purposes of the election of President and Vice President, to be electors appointed by a State; and they shall meet in the District and perform such duties as provided by the twelfth article of amendment.

Section 2.

The Congress shall have power to enforce this article by appropriate legislation.

AMENDMENT XXIV

Passed by Congress August 27, 1962. Ratified January 23, 1964

The right of citizens of the United States to vote in any primary or other election for President or Vice-President, for electors for President of Vice-President, or for Senator or Representative in Congress, shall not be denied or abridged by the United States or any State by reason of failure to pay poll tax or any other tax.

Section 2.

Congress shall have power to enforce this article by appropriate legislation.

AMENDMENT XXV

Passed by Congress July 6, 1965. Ratified February 10, 1967.

Section 1.

In case of the removal of the President from office or of his death or resignation, the Vice President shall become President.

Section 2.

Whenever there is a vacancy in the office of the Vice President, the President shall nominate a Vice President who shall take the office upon confirmation by a majority vote of both houses of Congress.

Section 3.

Whenever the President transmits to the President Pro tempore of the Senate and the Speaker of the House of Representatives his written declaration that he is unable to discharge the powers and duties of his office, and until he transmits to them a written declaration to the contrary, such powers and duties shall be discharged by the Vice President as Acting President.

Section 4.

Whenever the Vice President and a majority of either the principal officers of the executive departments or of such other body as Congress may by law provide, transmits to the President Pro tempore of the Senate and the Speaker of the House of Representatives their written declaration that the President is unable to discharge the powers and duties of his office, the Vice President shall immediately assume the powers and duties of the office as Acting President. Thereafter, when the President transmits to the President Pro tempore of the Senate and the Speaker of the House of Representatives his written declaration that no inability exists, he shall resume the powers and duties of his office unless the Vice President and a majority of either the principal officers of the executive departments or of such other body as Congress may by law provide, transmits within four days to the President Pro tempore of the Senate and the Speaker of the House of Representatives their written declaration that the President is unable to discharge the powers and duties of his office. Thereupon Congress shall decide the issue, assembling within forty-eight hours for that purpose if not in session. If the Congress, within twenty-one days after receipt of the latter written declaration, or, if Congress is not in session within twenty-one days after Congress is required to assemble, determines by two-thirds vote of both houses that the President is unable to discharge the powers and duties of his office, the Vice President shall continue to discharge the same as Acting President; otherwise, the President shall resume the powers and duties of his office.

AMENDMENT XXVI

Passed by Congress March 23, 1971. Ratified June 30, 171.

Section 1.

The right of citizens of the United States, who are 18 years of age or older, to vote shall not be denied or abridged by the United States or any state on account of age.

Section 2.

The Congress shall have power to enforce this article by appropriate legislation.

AMENDMENT XXVII

Passed by Congress September 25, 1789. Ratified May 7, 1992

No law, varying the compensation for the services of the Senators and Representatives shall take effect, until an election of Representatives shall have intervened.

Bibliography

Alderman, Ellen and Kennedy, Carolina. *In Our Defense: The Bill of Rights in Action*, William Morrow and Company, New York, 1991

Amar, Akhil Reed. *The Bill of Rights: Creation and Reconstruction*, Yale University Press, New Haven, 1998

Bancroft, George. *History of the Foundation of the Constitution of the United States*, Vol. 2. 2nd ed., D. Appleton and Company, New York, 1882

Beck, James M. *The Constitution of the United States: Yesterday, Today and Tomorrow?* George H. Doran Company, New York, 1924

Bowen, Catherine Drinkor. *Miracle at Philadelphia: The Story of the Constitutional Convention, 1787* Haymish Hamilton, London, 1966

Bradford, M. E. *A Worthy Company: Brief Lives of the Framers of the Constitution*, Plymouth Rock Foundation, Marlborough, New Hampshire, 1982

Brant, Irving. *James Madison: Father of the Constitution 1787–1800*, Bobbs-Merril Company, Indianapolis, 1950

Cogan, Neal H., ed. *The Complete Bill of Rights: The Drafts, Debates, Sources, and Origins*, Oxford University Press, New York, 1997

Dos Passos, John. *The Men Who Made the Nation*, Doubleday & Company, Inc., Garden City, New York, 1957

Farish, Leah. *The First Amendment: Freedom of Speech, Religion, and the Press*, Enslow Publishers, Inc., Springfield, New Jersey, 1998

Feinberg, Barbara Silberdick. *The Articles of Confederation: The First Constitution of the United States* Twenty-First Century Books, Brookfield, Connecticut, 2002

Kammen, Michael, ed. *The Origin of the American Constitution: A Documentary History*, Penguin Books, New York, 1986

Kelly, Alfred H. and Harbison, Wilfred A. *The American Constitution: Its Origins and Development*, W.W. Norton & Company, Inc., New York, 1970

Lieberman, Jethro K. *The Evolving Constitution*, Random House, New York, 1992

Mitchell, Broadus, and Mitchell, Louise Pearson. *A Biography of the Constitution of the United States*, Oxford University Press, 1964

Monk, Linda R. *The Bill of Rights: A User Guide,* Close Up Publishers, Alexandria, Virginia 1991

Morin, Isobel. *Our Changing Constitution: How and Why We Have Amended It,* The Millbrook Press, Brookfield, Connecticut, 1998

Rossiter, Clinton. *Alexander Hamilton and the Constitution,* Harcourt, Brace & World, New York, 1964

St. John, Jeffrey. *Constitutional Journal: Correspondent's Report from the Convention of 1787,* Jameson Books, Inc., Ottawa, Illinois, 1997

Schwartz, Bernard. *The Bill of Rights: A Documentary History,* Chelsea House, New York, 1971

Sunstein, Cass R. *The Partial Constitution,* Harvard University Press, Cambridge, Massachusetts, 1993

Warren, Charles. *The Making of the Constitution,* Harvard University Press, Cambridge, Massachusetts, 1937; Barnes & Noble, Inc., New York, 1967

ABOUT THE AUTHOR

Henry T. Conserva has taught in the public schools of California for over fifty years. He has been a curriculum specialist in social studies for the San Francisco Unified School District and has taught student teachers at San Francisco State University. He has done postgraduate study at Tel Aviv University in Israel, Harvard's Japan Institute and Oxford University in the U.K. He is the author of *Earth Tales, Propaganda Techniques, Tips for Teachers* and the *Illustrated Dictionary of Physical Geography*.